Kobe University Monograph Series in Social Science Research

The Kobe University Monograph Series in Social Science Research is an exciting interdisciplinary collection of monographs, both authored and edited, that encompass scholarly research not only in the economics but also in law, political science, business and management, accounting, international relations, and other sub-disciplines within the social sciences. As a national university with a special strength in the social sciences, Kobe University actively promotes interdisciplinary research. This series is not limited only to research emerging from Kobe University's faculties of social sciences but also welcomes cross-disciplinary research that integrates studies in the arts and sciences.

Kobe University, founded in 1902, is the second oldest national higher education institution for commerce in Japan and is now a preeminent institution for social science research and education in the country. Currently, the social sciences section includes four faculties—Law, Economics, Business Administration, and International Cooperation Studies—and the Research Institute for Economics and Business Administration (RIEB). There are some 230-plus researchers who belong to these faculties and conduct joint research through the Center for Social Systems Innovation and the Organization for Advanced and Integrated Research, Kobe University. This book series comprises academic works by researchers in the social sciences at Kobe University as well as their collaborators at affiliated institutions, Kobe University alumni and their colleagues, and renowned scholars from around the world who have worked with academic staff at Kobe University. Although traditionally the research of Japanese scholars has been publicized mainly in the Japanese language, Kobe University strives to promote publication and dissemination of works in English in order to further contribute to the global academic community.

More information about this series at https://link.springer.com/bookseries/16115

Katsuhiko Kokubu · Kimitaka Nishitani ·
Hirotsugu Kitada · Mitsunobu Ando

Emergent Responsible Management

A Social Connection Model

Springer

Katsuhiko Kokubu
Graduate School of Business Administration
Kobe University
Kobe, Hyogo, Japan

Kimitaka Nishitani
Research Institute for Economics and Business Administration (RIEB)
Kobe University
Kobe, Hyogo, Japan

Hirotsugu Kitada
Faculty of Business Administration
Hosei University
Chiyoda, Tokyo, Japan

Mitsunobu Ando
CSR Communication Association
Shinjuku, Tokyo, Japan

ISSN 2524-504X ISSN 2524-5058 (electronic)
Kobe University Monograph Series in Social Science Research
ISBN 978-981-19-0415-8 ISBN 978-981-19-0416-5 (eBook)
https://doi.org/10.1007/978-981-19-0416-5

Translation from the Japanese language edition: 創発型責任経営新しいつながりの経営モデル by Katsuhiko Kokubu et al., © The Authors 2019. Published by Nikkei Publishing Inc. All Rights Reserved.

This Springer imprint is published by the registered company Springer Nature Singapore Pte Ltd.
The registered company address is: 152 Beach Road, #21-01/04 Gateway East, Singapore 189721, Singapore

Preface*

How do you think of 'responsibility' in an organisation? You may consider it as something mainly assigned by your superior, from which you may be released if you fulfil it or blamed if not. The word 'responsibility' can be divided into 'response' and 'ability'. If you have the ability to respond to others' call, you have an obligation to respond. This is the original meaning of responsibility.

However, in the business world, 'responsibility' is understood as a sort of contract under which we may be released when we discharge it but blamed if we fail. This is a structural phenomenon caused by the fact that the economy, a core aspect of business, can only exist in a finite world. Therefore, most business responsibility is limited to laws, contracts, rules, routines, and the like, performed as finite responsibility.

Nonetheless, responsibility should not be bound by the economy or the law, rather it is inherent in human nature. Even without economic merit or law enforcement, anyone is supposed to have the will to respond to the call of others, which should be the origin of responsibility. Moreover, unlike finite responsibility, if we understand responsibility like this, the next call will be heard as soon as the current one is responded. In other words, responsibility is connected with certain responsibility fulfilled, others follow. In this sense, the nature of responsibility is not finite but rather infinite.

However, most 'responsibility' in business is fragmented rather than connected. In such cases, even if some 'responsibility' is given, it will disappear as soon as it is fulfilled. Moreover, we tend to avoid taking any 'responsibility' not being imposed on us, or we may undermine the normal operation of the organisation. Undoubtedly, such finite 'responsibility' is necessary for organisational operations. However, human society cannot function well with such type of 'responsibility' alone. Rather, we are required to listen to the call of others and respond them, thus creating a connection of responsibility to transform our society beyond the scope of finite 'responsibility'. No human progress would have been possible without it.

---

* This original Japanese edition of the book was published in 2019 by Nikkei Publishing Inc. (renamed Nikkei Business Publications, Inc. from April, 2020). This English edition is being published by Springer in May 2022.

Given this, we can understand that the majority of current business activities are still far away from practising responsibility in its original sense. Clearly, finite 'responsibility' is important for the economy, and we do not deny its significance. However, we may forget the inherent significance of responsibility if solely emphasising on finite responsibility. It is not only a loss for the organisation but also a detriment to the people who work. How can we overcome this problem? This book addresses this issue by introducing a new management idea—*emergent responsible management*.

* * *

The first 20 years of the new millennium (the 2000s) is a period when companies were awakened to social responsibility, and corporate social responsibility (CSR) has become a theme of discourse. Governments and NGOs have widely recognised the importance of CSR, and investors have come to appreciate these activities. Thus, CSR has been established as a common corporate practice worldwide.

The global spread of the CSR concept has considerably changed corporate activities. Previously, it was widely recognised that corporate operations should be consistent with the law, but with the popularisation of CSR, companies became to realise that they must comply with social norms beyond the scope of the law. Regarding activities related to social contribution and environmental protection, companies began to manage these issues by setting key performance indicators (KPIs) and repeating plan-do-check-act (PDCA) cycles as general management practices, with results being disclosed in their voluntary report (*e.g.* sustainability reports).

Consequently, the more generalised the CSR becomes, the more it is integrated with the normal business. In addition to repeating the PDCA cycle, value creation, which is a concept very close to the core business, has recently become the central theme in CSR. However, if it were difficult to distinguish between CSR and the core business, responsibility would be gradually incorporated into economic activities.

As social problems caused by corporate activities are becoming more and more serious, companies are required to be more engaged in CSR activities. This is not only because companies are deeply involved in current global problems, such as poverty, human rights, environmental concerns, economic disparity, and financial instability, but also because such global problems cannot be addressed without the endeavour of companies, as they have become more influential than governments.

However, the problems are not limited to such obvious issues. The pathology of modern society has deeply influenced the innermost being of working people. The larger the company is, the more detailed the division of labour becomes, and the stricter the management is. Nevertheless, it is generally detrimental to the wholeness of human beings because the assigned work is often practised in an excessively fragmented way in current management, resulting in more and more people becoming upset mentally, as well as physically. CSR has been focusing on issues not only outside the company (e.g. environmental protection and philanthropy) but also inside the company (e.g. employees' health and wellbeing). However, under severe economic and social pressure, it appears that no effective measures have been taken to date.

It should be appreciated that CSR in the past 20 years has made great contribution to our economy and society, but it is unlikely that it will continue to work given current CSR activities. This is because CSR, which should have provided a chance for companies to open to society, has become simply a part of ordinary business, and there is a great decline in the willingness of companies to solve social issues. Along these lines, CSR may ultimately turn into an activity that protects companies from society.

To solve this problem, a fundamental shift in mind-set is required. We need to turn to the essential meaning of responsibility by starting to search for our own responsibility. Responsibility is supposed to be the ability to respond to the call of others; thus, it will essentially lead to an emergent act, where there is always an opportunity to change the organisation. This book explores the emergent theory and practice of management that pursues responsibility to deal with such problems.

* * *

This book is mainly divided into three parts. Part I includes a series of chapters (Chaps. 1–3) that reflect on some key concepts and elements that underpin the theory of emergent responsible management. The central concept is infinite responsibility. We argue that responsibility should be infinite instead of being limited in business, mainly based on the theories of modern philosophers Emanuel Levinas, Jacques Derrida, and even Iris Marion Young. In addition, when discussing responsibility in corporate management, it is necessary to be aware of 'emergence' as its essential element. Since emergent responsible management is an emergent practice that occurs between oneself and others, promoting such practice in an organisation requires some specific measures, including the establishment of corporate philosophy.

Part II of the book presents five companies' case studies. Emergent responsible management has already been practised by certain companies; thus, it is not simply a utopian dream. It should be noted that these companies' approach is not explicitly recognised as emergent responsible management as defined in this book since this is the first time we name it here. However, activities reflecting its fundamental elements have already been practised in many companies. This book studies five companies that are found suitable for emergent responsible management: OMRON (Chap. 4), Bridgestone (Chap. 5), Marui Group (Chap. 6), Yahoo Japan (Chap. 7) and Mitsubishi Heavy Industries Group (Chap. 8). Undoubtedly, there are multiple practical examples of emergent responsible management in many other companies, and we hope that you could read it while considering the activities of your own organisations.

In the last part of this book (Chaps. 9–12), we discuss the methods and effects of introducing emergent responsible management into practice. To encourage its continued practice in companies, the corresponding organisational design and operation processes are of great importance. Emergent responsible management is a new idea; thus, a specific design and related processes are yet to be developed. However, based on the case studies, we discuss the potentially practical design and processes as concretely as possible. In addition, we examine how emergent responsible management can be applied to fulfil the Sustainable Development Goals (SDGs). Although the SDGs are currently receiving much attention, emergent responsible management would be effective in reformulating these SDGs-related activities as enduring initiatives. Finally, an Afterword is added for a synopsis of the book, including answers to some questions you may have. If you have difficulty understanding the book or have any questions, please refer to the Afterword.

Another message conveyed in this book is about *connection*. If responsibility means the ability to respond to the call of others, it implies the creation of connection. The more you fulfil your responsibility, the more connections you will create. Emergent responsible management is a practice of making permanently growing connections with those outside one's company. This, in turn, leads to the sustainability of the organisation, which is also implied in the subtitle of this book *A Social Connection Model*.

In terms of connection, economic relation is also a kind of connection. However, the economy has limited scope and is only a part of various connections of human beings. Therefore, it is also necessary to consider a company's social connections. This is the ultimate purpose of emergent responsible management. Restoring such connections is of paramount importance now since companies have become the centre of human life. However, while the economy is part of society, society is not part of the economy.

This is a business book intended for people working in companies; thus, we have tried our best to make the explanation as simple as possible. While minimising citations from academic literature, we have tried to convey essential ideas compactly without undermining the theoretical insights. Therefore, for more academic discussions, please refer to the author's other papers and books.

* * *

The concept of applying infinite responsibility to corporate management was developed when I published *Beyond Accountability toward Management Ethics* (Yuikaku) in 2017, which mainly involved a theoretical discussion. I wanted to publish a practical version soon after that book. However, in the case of practical research, an individual researcher has limitations. Therefore, I talked to some senior and young researchers, Kimitaka Nishitani and Hirotsuga Kitada, with whom I have collaborated in many joint studies so far. Furthermore, the perspective of academia alone may be biased. Therefore, I also invited Mitsunobu Ando, who is a CSR consultant, to join the research. All of the four members from different generations were deeply engaged in a series of research activities, including research design meetings, fieldwork, result discussions, and manuscript reviews. Without these people's enthusiasm and commitment, this book simply would not have been possible. Thanks to my co-authors, the combination of theory and practice is much profounder than what I expected.

In writing this book, we were fortunate to receive support from a lot of people. In particular, we express our deepest gratitude to the five companies in this book. It is clear that the book would not have been written without the dedicated cooperation of these companies. We also thank many other companies that we visited during our research, although we could not take them up as company cases.

We are unable to mention everyone's name here, still, we would like to thank Satoshi Ando, Koki Kurokawa, Satomi Somekawa, Naoya Etani of OMRON Corporation; Kyoko Sasaki from Bridgestone Corporation; Tomohiro Niikura and Yuko Shiota of Marui Group; Koichi Sunaga, Takuya Hasegawa, and Yuya Matsumoto of Yahoo Japan Corporation; and Toshiya Ejima of Mitsubishi Hitachi Power Systems, Ltd. The progress of this study was reported at the Kobe CSR study group in Osaka and Tokyo. We also thank Masahiko Fujichika, Chairman of the Study Group, and Hirotaka Yanagita and Yuriko Nakao, Vice-Chairmen. In addition, Kazunori Amino of Nikkei Publishing Inc. provided valuable advice to us. For research support and proofreading, Kento Abe, a doctoral student from the Graduate School of Business Administration, Kobe University; Masako Onishi from the Research Support Office; and Mami Iwanaga of Kokubu Laboratory also helped significantly. We express our great appreciation to them.

In writing this book, we were fortunate to have financial support from Kobe University Research Institute of Economics and Business Administration, the 100th anniversary of foundation, Kobe University System Innovation Center, Kobe University Strategic Project 'Building Future Century Urbanology by Advanced Research of Fusion of Humanities and Scientists', JSPS KAKENHI (19H01547, 19H01549, 18H03824, 18K12902, 16H03679, 16H03006), Research and Development Fund for Environmental Reconstruction and Conservation/Environmental Research (JPMEERF16S11606), and Melco Science Foundation.

This book is not the end, but just the beginning of our research. We hope to connect with those who are interested in it and spread the concept of emergent responsible management to the world.

Kobe, Japan
May 2019

Katsuhiko Kokubu

The original version of the book was revised: Belated corrections received in Chapters 1, 2, 9 and 11 have been updated. The correction to the book is available at https://doi.org/10.1007/978-981-19-0416-5_13

Contents

About the Authors

Katsuhiko Kokubu is a Professor at the Graduate School of Business Administration, Kobe University, Japan. He is currently serving as a Dean of the Graduate School of Business Administration. He was also a Vice President of Kobe University from 2019 to 2021. He completed his Ph.D. in Business Administration at Osaka City University. Professor Kokubu is a leading scholar of sustainable management and accounting. He has published more than 30 books, including *Sustainability Management and Business Strategy in Asia* (World Scientific, 2019) and 300 papers in leading journals including the *Journal of Cleaner Production, Journal of Environmental Management,* and *Sustainable Production and Consumption.*

Kimitaka Nishitani is a Professor at the Research Institute for Economics and Business Administration (RIEB), Kobe University. He is also currently serving as the Deputy Director of the RIEB and the Center for Computational Social Science, Kobe University. He completed his Ph.D. in Business Administration at Kobe University. He was also an academic visitor at the School of Management, Royal Holloway, University of London, from 2015 to 2016. Professor Nishitani has published extensively on sustainability management, and social and environmental reporting in leading journals including *Journal of Cleaner Production, Journal of Environmental Management,* and *Sustainable Production and Consumption.*

Hirotsugu Kitada is an Associate Professor of the Faculty of Business Administration, Hosei University, Japan. He completed his Ph.D. in Business Administration at Kobe University. In 2012, he joined the Faculty of Business Administration, Hosei University as an associate professor and is concurrently an invited researcher at KDDI Research, Inc. He is also an expert for ISO/TC323 (Circular Economy) and, as well, was an expert for ISO/TC207 (ISO14007, Guidelines for Determining Environmental Costs and Benefits). His research interests encompass management accounting and sustainability accounting. His work has been published in leading journals including *PLOS ONE* and the *Journal of Cleaner Production.*

Mitsunobu Ando is a representative director of the CSR Communication Association. After obtaining his bachelor's degree at Daito Bunka University, he worked for an internet advertising company for several years. In 2008, he became an independent consultant and has provided consulting services to listed companies regarding sustainability management in such areas as strategy formulation, third-party evaluation, web/report creation support, and information disclosure.

Chapter 1
Responsibility Creates Value in Management

Katsuhiko Kokubu

Abstract Whereas the concept of responsibility of corporation has been brought to the forefront with the increasing divergence of companies' pursuit of private interest and public interest, its essence has not been fully recognised. In particular, the term of CSR has been widely used so far, but the inherent nature of responsibility is far beyond the scope of traditional CSR. Meanwhile, the lack of understanding in responsibility has inevitably brought about the restrictive feeling associated with organisational CSR activities. The present chapter aims to revisit the essential meaning of responsibility by tracing back the history of CSR and investigating how the concept of responsibility has been explored and developed in CSR. In so doing, we claim that the inherent nature of responsibility is infinite so that the business is required, even partially, to be operated under infinite responsibility and then create shared value. To this aim, we propose emergent responsible management to bring out activities based on infinite responsibility and the rest of the book provides theoretical and practical insights on how to develop such a new management tool.

1.1 Companies and Responsibility

The relationship between companies and responsibility has been discussed since the birth of modern corporations. Capitalism is basically designed on the assumption that the pursuit of private interests will eventually lead to public good. However, since activities for the pursuit of private interests are not the same as those for the public's interest, there is no perfect agreement between private and public interests. Thus, addressing the problems arising from this divergence has been necessary. The most fundamental means to achieve this is through government regulations of companies. The government is supposed to protect public interests by restricting the behaviours of private companies through laws and regulations.

However, as capitalism evolves and the market economy spreads worldwide, government regulations gradually lose their effectiveness, and companies are

---

The original version of this chapter was revised: Belated corrections received in Chapters 1, 2, 9 and 11 have been updated. The correction to this chapter is available at https://doi.org/10.1007/978-981-19-0416-5_13

K. Kokubu et al., *Emergent Responsible Management*, Kobe University Monograph Series in Social Science Research, https://doi.org/10.1007/978-981-19-0416-5_1

explicitly required to take responsibility for society voluntarily. The modern wave of such a movement began in the twenty-first century in the European Union (EU), where CSR has been taken voluntarily by companies as a policy and CSR has become widely used globally since then. In other words, CSR has not been confined to Europe but rather it has become common worldwide. In Japan, CSR began booming as early as in 2003, known as 'the first year of CSR'.

Today, after 20 years of the above initiatives, the concept of CSR has been recognised as one of the essential components of the business, regardless of the size or geographic locations. However, concerning the definition of CSR, there is no common understanding as to whether CSR is the same as compliance, engagement in philanthropy, environmental preservation activities, volunteering, or social value creation initiatives. The term CSR is so widely used that it is too difficult to recognise its essence. If a company's purpose in engaging in CSR is to contribute to the main business or to enhance its reputation, then that is not responsibility to society but responsibility to the company, which is contradictory to the original concept of CSR. Unfortunately, many people working in the business are not aware of this.

Meanwhile, if CSR activities have been continued for many years, such activities will slow down and become monotonous. Compliance is basically routine work and for other activities like environmental conservation, the longer it continues, the lesser is the chance for reducing environmental burden given the same volume of business activities. As a result, more and more companies are struggling in search of relevant topics for the CSR report published annually. As these companies consider CSR as merely compliance with laws and regulations, the additional information disclosed to outsiders will decrease. Nevertheless, many guidelines do not clearly answer the basic question of why disclosing CSR information to the outsiders is fundamentally important.

The restrictive feeling associated with CSR activities is not something new; any organisation may feel the same way after their engagement in CSR for a few years. The idea of creating shared values (CSV) has emerged as a breakthrough idea since mid-2000s. The slogan that matches the company's original purpose of value creation has attracted many companies. In Japan, these companies started one after another renaming their CSR department as CSV department. However, as the concept of *shared value* is somewhat ambiguous, it is often difficult to understand the real meaning.

Recently, the sustainable development goals (SDGs) adopted by the United Nations in 2015 have received significant attention from businesses, but only to link the existing CSR activities to these SDGs is almost meaningless. Engagement in SDGs is a huge opportunity to revitalise CSR. However, if we are not able to do it innovatively, we will soon realise that the activities are just the same as before.

The root cause of the problem involved with CSR is the lack of understanding of the most fundamental concept—*responsibility*. Even international CSR-related documents or guidelines define responsibility so generally that it can be applied to any activity. This might be inevitable during the initial spreading stage of the CSR concept. After 20 years, we have already gained a lot of experience in CSR and thus, it is the time to revisit its essential meaning and look forward to the future.

The original meaning of *responsibility* should be understood from its root words, *response* and *ability*. To respond, we must answer to the call of others. Think about where others are (not limited to humans or those who are living at this moment), what they are calling for and how we can respond to their call—responsibility is all about such activities.[1] However, many CSR activities nowadays are decided at the beginning of the year, with results reported in the end of the year. Thus, such activities are far from the essence of responsibility.

Responsibility is essentially a spontaneous, active, and emergent concept. Responding to the call of others is an obligation, but it cannot be linked to activities without considering how to, and who will, respond. If this call is answered, another new call will emerge by connecting oneself to others. Moreover, being able to respond to the call of others brings something valuable to others. Thus, fulfilling responsibility and value creation should happen simultaneously. As such, it is not necessary to recognise the difference between CSR and CSV; rather, both of them must be operated in the same manner. However, it is difficult to ensure such agreement between CSR and CSV under current practices. Therefore, it is required to convert CSR into active and spontaneous activities by employees.

To do so, the stereotype of CSR must be overcome. The term CSR itself has helped spread the concept itself to the world, but after nearly 20 years the related activities have become limited. Since the scope of inherent responsibility cannot be defined in advance, the area of CSR should not be constant either.

Therefore, in this book, we name management based on responsibility in its original meaning as emergent responsible management and explore the possibility from both theoretical and practical perspectives. To do so, it is indispensable to understand the meaning of responsibility correctly. In this chapter, we highlight the limitations of CSR, review its history, and argue that it is necessary to return to the original meaning of responsibility.

1.2 The Birth of CSR

As mentioned earlier, the modern concept of CSR came into birth in the EU in 2000. The European Commission defined CSR in a green paper published in 2001 as 'a concept whereby companies integrate social and environmental concerns in their business operations and in their interaction with their stakeholders on a voluntary basis'.[2] The EU member states adopted the promotion of CSR as a policy, and

---

[1] The background of such an idea is a philosophical debate on the responsibility of Emmanuel Levinas and Jacques Derrida, which is one of the representative ideas in modern philosophy. We will discuss some of their theoretical viewpoints in Chap. 2. For more details, see Kokubu, K. (2017) *Beyond Accountability toward Management Ethics*, Yuikaku (in Japanese).

[2] Commission of the European Communities, Green paper: Promoting a European Framework for Corporate Social Responsibility, DOC01/9.

even CSR ministers were appointed in some countries such as the United Kingdom and France.

The EU adopted CSR as a policy against the background of neoliberal economics and policies, including deregulation, a strong belief in market force and a small government. As a result, the problem of how to deal with social and environmental issues that cannot be tackled with market discipline came up. Traditionally, these issues were supposed to be subject to government regulations, but the strengthening of such regulations conflicted with the aforesaid neoliberal policies. Meanwhile, social and environmental problems were transforming from individual problems, such as conventional labour issues or pollution prevention, to very complicated global problems based on the diversification of values. Complex issues like climate change, biodiversity, and so on that could not be addressed through direct regulations became severe and more visible.

Under such circumstances, new policies of encouraging companies to solve these problems voluntarily emerged instead of directly regulating companies' behaviours that cause social and environmental problems. CSR is one of these policies. Therefore, CSR in the twenty-first century is a concept that is fundamentally different from compliance or philanthropy, and it is not the same as the previous concept of CSR in the 1970s, which mainly focused on pollution and human rights issues. Such a policy shift was advantageous for companies due to deregulation, and thus, CSR was supported by economic associations.

While CSR is a policy choice by the European Union, social and environmental issues have been globally recognised and driven by the responsible investment movement, CSR immediately diffused among the international community. Following the same wave, Japan experienced a boom of CSR in 2003, which is called 'the first year of CSR in Japan. However, unlike in the European Union, the CSR policy in Japan has not been explicitly defined, and compliance or philanthropy has not been clearly distinguished from CSR.

Since CSR basically involves companies' voluntary activities, the systems designed for it need to be supported by the private sectors rather than the government. Two remarkable standards were set at the beginning and the end of the 2000s: the Global Reporting Initiative (GRI) *Sustainability Reporting Guidelines* (currently *the Sustainability Reporting Standard*) and ISO 26000 *Guidance on Social Responsibility*. GRI guidelines are used for preparing sustainability reports and nowadays, they have become a de-facto standard for multinational companies. Meanwhile, ISO26000 presents the overall picture of an organisation's social responsibility.

In both GRI guidelines and ISO26000, the relationship between stakeholders and companies is the focal point. As CSR is a voluntary activity, the involvement of external stakeholders is essential to ensure its legitimacy. Instead of being regulated by the government, a scheme in which CSR activities are overseen through the active stakeholder engagement in corporate management has been established in the CSR world.

1.3 The Restrictive Feeling Associated with CSR and the Emergence of CSV

As mentioned above, CSR spread worldwide during the 2000s and was recognised as an important issue. It has been embedded into regular business activities in developed countries, as well as in developing countries. As a voluntary activity, it only means that companies can determine what to do and to what extent with CSR. They do not have any option to refuse to take actions as long as something is recognised as responsibility. Therefore, companies are required to set CSR goals, promote activities and construct the plan-do-check-act (PDCA) cycle if possible. If the target is to solve a specific environmental or social problem, it is not necessary to continue the activities once the problem is solved. However, problems, such as climate change or the conservation of biodiversity, that require continuous improvement cannot be figured out very easily, are the central issues of current CSR.

Therefore, CSR needs to be considered as an issue that should be embedded in the continuous operation of a company. However, companies soon realise the difficulty in implementing such PDCA cycle on CSR at the same level as regular business activities, where there is a visible goal, that is, earning profits. Whatever efforts they make, it is impossible to fully eliminate environmental burden, and the promotion of diversity only progresses gradually. Hence, maintaining employees' motivation to practise CSR for the long term is particularly difficult.

This is the same as in the preparation of a sustainability report that discloses the results of CSR activities. It is sufficient to only explain the financial statement and earning performance in annual financial reports. However, it is normal that similar CSR activities are repeated every year, which makes the report quite alike as well. Due to the annual issuance of CSR reports, companies run out of content that is new enough to attract the attention of stakeholders. In recent years, responsible investment has expanded and the importance of sustainability information disclosure has been acknowledged. Nevertheless, only a few companies recognise that investors need sustainability information, but many companies still do not fully understand the purpose of issuing CSR reports.

In other words, while CSR has been perceived as an indispensable activity for companies and has spread worldwide in the twenty-first century, it has become apparent that people engaged in CSR start feeling restricted as they continue their CSR activities every year. However, CSV is the concept that has brought a new perspective of value creation into the world of CSR and provided an avenue to overcome this situation. CSV is an activity that has been practised by Nestlé since the 2000s. It is a way of thinking aimed at creating a common social value among different sectors in the society. CSV has been noted remarkably since it was developed theoretically by Michael Porter, a famous professor of Harvard Business School. Since then, creating value has emerged as a central concept in CSR. Porter and his colleagues argue that while CSR is only a good deed, CSV is the joint initiative for creating shared values with other sectors and thus, they place CSV at the centre of corporate activities.[3]

The concept of CSV has been very easy for companies to accept because reducing environmental burden alone does not increase the motivation of many employees, but creating value is consistent with pursuing economic value in the main business. Moreover, if the creation of social value offers business opportunities, it is beneficial for companies as well. In response to such development, the European Union has redefined CSR at the 10th anniversary by incorporating CSR into policy issues, redefining the purpose of CSR as 'maximising the creation of shared value for their owners/shareholders and for their other stakeholders and society at large'.[4]

Since then, the idea of placing value creation at the centre of CSR has spread worldwide, and in 2013 the IIRC (International Integrated Reporting Council) released the *International Integrated Report < IR > Framework*, which called for reporting on value creation through six capitals (i.e., financial, manufactured, intellectual, human, social and relationship, and natural capital). Thus, the creation of social value as shared value has become the focus in CSR. In addition, since value creation is the focus of corporate activities, it is increasingly necessary to integrate CSR into corporate strategies. The number of companies publishing integrated reports has been increasing and reporting that focus on value creation in CSR has become popular worldwide, including in Japan.

1.4 Criticism of CSV

CSV has spread as a new way of thinking about CSR, and in Japan, some companies have changed their CSR departments to CSV departments. In the CSR report, the term CSV appears frequently, and the number of companies aiming to create social value has increased. However, there is criticism that CSV is not the same as CSR. For example, the Asia–Pacific Human Rights Information Center (HURIGHTS OSAKA) and the CSO Network published *Principles on CSR and CSV* in 2014, claiming that CSR cannot be substituted by CSV, and it is necessary to verify whether the value created by CSV is equal to *social value*, thereby questioning the trend of emphasising CSV.

[3] Porter, M. E. and Kramer, M. R. (2006) Strategy and Society: The link between competitive advantage and corporate social responsibility, *Harvard Business Review*, December.

Porter, M. E. and Kramer, M. R. (2011) Creating Shared Value: How to Reinvent Capitalism – and Unleash a Wave of Innovation and Growth, *Harvard Business Review*, January–February.

[4] European Commission (2011) *Communication from the Commission to the European Parliament, the Council, the European Economic and Social Committee and the Committee of the Regions: A Renewed EU Strategy 2011–14 for Corporate Social Responsibility*, COM (2011) 681, p.6.

Meanwhile, many companies that have set up a CSV department are struggling to create shared values. In the case of Nestlé, they successfully defined CSV as part of their global business. However, in general, if a company promotes CSV as a business activity, it is difficult to differentiate it from its main business. On the contrary, if they limit it within the scope of the CSR, value creation becomes difficult.

As mentioned above, the IIRC < *IR* > *Framework* requires the value creation process through six types of capital be disclosed as a business model in the integrated report. However, not many companies that issued the so-called integrated reports have fully met this requirement. Even if they seem to disclose some relevant information, in most cases, it is merely transforming the environmental performance or social performance into the form of value creation through the six types of capital indicated by the framework. In essence, it is not value creation but simply a rework of CSR.

In fact, it is difficult for companies to pursue CSV because there is no mechanism for creating social value in companies. Although some of the individual initiatives can be taken up as 'special topics' in the CSR report, they cannot be incorporated systematically in management. Unlike Nestlé, it is difficult to explain what is different from the main business simply by understanding CSV in an abstract way. It may lead to criticism from external stakeholders who are trying to keep companies socially responsible.

This problem stems from trying to separate CSR, CSV, and economic activities, which is very difficult. Meanwhile, positioning CSR and CSV as a means of economic activities contradicts with creating shared value with society and corporate responsibility. Therefore, to promote these activities, a deep understanding of the concept of responsibility in CSR is necessary to organise and restructure the relationships of these three areas.

1.5 Meaning of Responsibility in CSR

While CSR has spread as a common term in corporate society throughout the twenty-first century, responsibility as the core concept has not been sufficiently studied. If the understanding of the concept of responsibility is ambiguous, the argument for CSR will always conflict with economic activities. The fundamental reason why CSR and CSV are confused with each other is that CSR and CSV are both easily understood as a means of business.

Along with justice and ethics, the concept of responsibility is a central issue in philosophy. According to modern philosophy, 'responsibility' is about obligation to others. The word 'response', as a root word of 'responsibility' suggests that 'responsibility' primarily means responsiveness to others. However, the connotation that responsibility depends on others presents a very difficult problem in practice. Various inconveniences would occur in conducting organisational activities if the scope of responsibility could not be determined by practitioners themselves alone.

In business, economic responsibility is fundamental, and current corporate systems (e.g. limited liability company) have been designed to limit the scope of 'responsibility', where accountability is also necessary. Accountability is generally understood as being requested to explain something with the possibility of receiving some sanctions[5] (including not only negative sanctions but also positive rewards) if the request is not fulfilled, and this concept of accountability prevails in corporate activities. Accountability is considered to exist when any explanation is required for certain actions even if not specified in any document.

The element of responsiveness in 'responsibility' connotes being open to others, but accountability needs to be limited. Without finite accountability, the business activities cannot be carried out. Thus, it is natural that corporate responsibilities are formulated as matters of accountability. However, the problem is that not all responsibility can be set as finite accountability. This leaves some areas where no one is responsible for, which is the root cause of environmental and social issues, as well as other types of risk. If CSR should be designed to overcome this, then the related responsibility should not be limited.

As long as the responsibility is for others, the scope of responsibility cannot be defined by oneself. Thus, responsibility is essentially infinite. This seems as if there would be tremendous responsibility, but it is not true since infinity cannot be quantified and has no concept of magnitude. Rather, infinite responsibility means an attitude to the world, believing that everything may be our own responsibility. Theoretically, since others have the same infinite responsibility as we do, our own responsibility is also the responsibility of others, and then, if infinite responsibility is shared in the society, the responsibility attached to some specific individuals would not exist.

To be clear, infinite responsibility is not the same as expanded responsibility. The infinity of responsibility, as the philosopher Emmanuel Levinas says, increases as it is fulfilled.[6] Increasing responsibility means searching for tasks to be fulfilled one after another and thus, the responsibility is connected infinitely.

1.6 Responsibility Creates Value

If the responsibility in CSR is regarded as infinite, CSR should be redefined as a practice through which companies seek their own responsibility. Certainly, it is not realistic to formulate all corporate activities under infinite responsibility. Without economic responsibility being limited in scope, running daily business operations will be impossible. However, if the essence of responsibility becomes infinite, it would be necessary to secure a space (somehow) for infinite responsibility that is beyond finite accountability in a company.

---

[5] Bovens, M. (2007) Analysing assessing accountability: A conceptual framework, *European Law Journal*, 13(4).

[6] Levinas, E. (1979) *Totality and Infinity: An Essay on Exteriority*, (translated by Lingis, A.) Martinus NijiHoff Publishers, The Hague, Netherland.

Levinas, E. (1981) *Otherwise than Being or beyond Essence*, (translated by Lingis, A.) Martinus NijiHoff Publishers, The Hague, Netherland.

Then who should be responsible for infinite responsibility in companies? There is no one other than every individual who belongs to the company. A company is lifeless, which cannot take responsibility by nature, thus only humans can discharge it. Responsibility does not rise unless each person acts spontaneously. Therefore, responsibility is inherently a subjective concept and, in fact, manifests itself as an active and emergent action. Since responsibility is to respond to the call of others, if certain requirements are fulfilled, some value will be created. Thus, discharging the responsibility to others is synonymous with creating value for others.

However, one's self is also another person to others, so others also have responsibility to one's self. Therefore, if oneself could fulfil his/her own responsibility to others, others would also fulfil their own responsibility for oneself, and then the value would be created for both parties. If an organisation like a company could take such behaviour, it would create value for others, and others would simultaneously create value for it.

The IIRC < *IR* > *Framework* illustrates this relationship as shown in Fig. 1.1. The value created for others will also increase value for the organisation. The greater the value created for others, the greater the value created for the organisation. This (although merely an image) indicates that when recognising responsibility to others as the creation of value, the effects are always reciprocal.

This figure represents the essence of the corporation because it is a mechanism that creates value for others (stakeholders) by satisfying their needs and gains benefits for the organisation thereby. Therefore, CSR and CSV can be understood as essentially the same concept. Based on this understanding, activities such as compliance and the like should be distinguished from CSR.

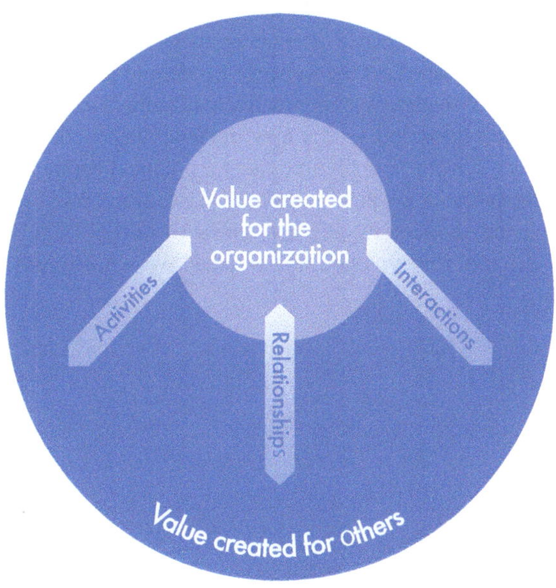

Fig. 1.1 The concept of value creation in the IIRC < IR > Framework. *Source* IIRC (2013) *The International Framework*, p. 10

However, it is not realistic to carry out all the economic activities in a company based on the principle of infinite responsibility. Management is charged with economic responsibility. Since the economic benefit is measurable, it does not match with the concept of infinity. Without the principle of finite responsibility, management cannot carry out economic or organisational activities. However, running corporate activities solely based on the principle of economic responsibility is also difficult because of the inherent nature of human beings. The point is how to embed infinite responsibility into corporate management and activities to solve this problem.

Therefore, the difference between CSR (which is equal to CSV) and economic activities is whether responsibility is infinite or not. In principle, corporate management is carried out under finite responsibility, but the inherent nature of responsibility is infinite so that the business is required, even partially, to be operated under infinite responsibility and then create shared value. Without such understanding, CSR and CSV would lose their inherent meaning in corporate management. If we consider CSR and CSV as a means of implementing economic activities, this is fundamentally paradoxical. However, we should understand that implementing CSR might create economic value for a company as an unexpected gain. We should not expect any benefit for ourselves before conducting CSR. In other words, CSR comes the first and the benefit for oneselves is the second. This order determines the ethic itself.

Activities based on this inherent concept of responsibility are beyond the scope of traditional CSR. Undoubtedly, management that is based on infinite responsibility reflects the true CSR, but if it is called CSR, it will be confused with the CSR that had already become widespread. For activities based on infinite responsibility, it is critically important for each employee to act spontaneously, and this is an emergent practice that is created through interactions with others. This goes beyond the scope of traditional CSR. In this book, this type of management is named emergent responsible management, which can be defined as management that encourages spontaneous activities by employees based on the concept of infinite responsibility and creates emergent practices. Consequently, this practice naturally leads to new connections.

How can a company develop such a new management model? This book seeks to address this question from both theoretical and practical perspectives. To do so, it is necessary to clarify the concept of infinite responsibility first, and it is important to understand that the spontaneity and activeness of human beings, as well as the emergence brought about by practice, are crucial. We will discuss these points in Chaps. 2 and 3.

Chapter 2
Beyond Accountability, Towards Responsibility

Katsuhiko Kokubu

Abstract This chapter provides a comprehensive discussion of infinite responsibility by distinguishing responsibility from accountability. Along with the expansion of accountability in modern society, it is necessary to restore infinite responsibility as not all of the problems could be solved by accountability alone. It points out that management needs to coordinate organisational behaviour so that both responsibility and accountability can function well within the organisation. CSR has been originally designed as a concept for such intention, but it has not always successfully dealt with infinite responsibility so far. It is necessary to be free from the stereotype of traditional CSR and emergent responsible management is advocated as a practical solution to cover the entire corporate management.

2.1 Responsibility and Accountability

The first step in promoting emergent responsible management is to create a system that pursues infinite responsibility for the business. To this end it is necessary to distinguish responsibility from accountability. Furthermore, management needs to coordinate organisational behaviour so that both responsibility and accountability can function well within the organisation.

To simply define these two concepts in this book, accountability is a kind of obligation, of which the contents to be fulfilled is defined on some basis, and the fulfilment and termination can be objectively recognised. Here, 'some basis' means that certain liability is prescribed by contracts, rules, and so on, and certain sanctions will be imposed if not fulfilled. Sanctions can include informal types, such as social sanctions, as well as rewards for achievements beyond commitment in some cases.

Meanwhile, responsibility in this book literally means the ability to respond to the call of others and is based on subjective judgments as to what we are able to and should do for others. It is not something that can be identified by contract or rules.

The original version of this chapter was revised: Belated corrections received in Chapters 1, 2, 9 and 11 have been updated. The correction to this chapter is available at https://doi.org/10.1007/978-981-19-0416-5_13

K. Kokubu et al., *Emergent Responsible Management*, Kobe University Monograph Series in Social Science Research, https://doi.org/10.1007/978-981-19-0416-5_2

Therefore, it cannot be compelled, and it should depend on the spontaneous actions of individuals.

On the other hand, accountability must be set artificially, while responsibility comes from within one's self, thus they are fundamentally different. A small organisation, such as a family, might be able to operate with only responsibility, but this might not be possible in the case of large organisations, including corporations and governments. As a result, accountability as a means of assigning 'responsibility' has been created to meet organisational and social management needs.

From this perspective, we can say that companies are established within a net of accountability. Performing day-to-day duties is the fulfilment of individual accountability, and if any quota is imposed based on the quality of the results, accountability will be enhanced accordingly. A company consists of a chain of the accountability of subordinates to superiors, with the CEO at the top, who also has accountability to the shareholders. Thus, accountability forms a hierarchical organisation by flowing vertically from subordinates to superiors, from supervisors to top management, and from top management to shareholders. This is exactly the same for administrative organisations.

However, since responsibility is subjective, it has no specific direction, and the range is not limited; therefore, responsibility is infinite in this sense, which is fundamentally different from accountability as finite responsibility. Responsibility, as exemplified by the feelings of parents towards children, is originally derived from human emotions.

Therefore, it is not possible to operate a large organisation, such as a corporation or a government, with only responsibility in its original meaning of infinite responsibility, which may cause significant inefficiency because responsibility cannot be enforced in principle. Therefore, in modern society, the governing system has been formed with accountability instead of responsibility. When we feel that the use of discretion is restricted in our workplace, this may be because accountability has replaced responsibility.

The expansion of accountability is inevitable in modern society, but if it reduces the scope of responsibility, it would not only impair humanity's wholeness but also raise various social problems. Many of the social and environmental issues we are facing nowadays are those where no one has been previously held accountable. Externality, a concept of economics, is exactly a good example of this.

Expanding accountability is an essential requirement for the establishment of modern society, but we also face problems that cannot be solved with only accountability. It seems that modern society is trying to survive with the further expansion of accountability, but this strategy has limitations. Along with the expansion of accountability, it is also necessary to restore infinite responsibility. Thus, emergent responsible management is advocated as a practical solution. Originally, this problem should have been tackled within activities in CSR, but until now, CSR has not always successfully dealt with infinite responsibility as we explained above.

2.2 Responsibility and Accountability in ISO 26000

As mentioned in Chap. 1, CSR was adopted as a policy agenda by the European Union in the 2000s and gained attention worldwide since then. Many international and national organisations, have established various standards and guidelines for CSR, but the most systematically compiled document at the international level is ISO 26000—*Guidance on Social Responsibility.*[1]

The ISO began to develop CSR standards shortly after the announcement of the EU policy. The standardisation on CSR by ISO has attracted the attention of many countries and involved experts from over 90 national and 40 regional organisations. After nearly 10 years of discussion, ISO 26000 was issued in 2010. This document offered essential insights on global CSR at that time. In this section, we track the ISO 26000 to see how the concepts of responsibility and accountability are understood in the CSR world.

According to ISO 26000, accountability is defined as the 'state of being answerable for decisions and activities to the organization's governing bodies, legal authorities and, more broadly, its stakeholders (ISO26000, Section 2.1)'. Meanwhile, responsibility is not explained as an individual term but as being defined in social responsibility as follows.

> Responsibility of an organization for the impacts of its decisions and activities on society and the environment, through transparent and ethical behaviour that
>
> —contributes to sustainable development, including health and the welfare of society;
>
> —takes into account the expectations of stakeholders;
>
> —is in compliance with applicable law and consistent with international norms of behaviour; and
>
> —is integrated throughout the organisation and practiced in its relationships (ISO26000, Section 2.18).

Thus, in ISO 26000, accountability is defined as obligation to explain, and responsibility is understood as an obligation to take some action. The definition of responsibility above implies compliance with laws and international norms, which is different from the idea of infinite responsibility. Responsibility must go beyond legal compliance.[2] However, ISO 26000 also provides a deeper understanding of social responsibility and accountability as follows:

> The essential characteristic of social responsibility is the willingness of an organization to incorporate social and environmental considerations in its decision-making and be accountable for the impacts of its decisions and activities on society and the environment (ISO26000, Section 3.3.1)

The important point to emphasise here is that responsibility contains the element of *willingness*, which illustrates well the spontaneous nature of responsibility. It is also

---

[1] The title is *Social Responsibility* instead of *Corporate Social Responsibility* because it covers social responsibility that is common to all organisations, not just companies.

[2] Derrida, J. (1992) Force of Law: The "Mystical Foundation of Authority", in Cornell, D., Rosenfeld, M. and Carlson, D. G. (eds.) *Deconstruction and the Possibility of Justice*, Routledge.

important to point out that responsibility is a concept that embraces accountability by claiming willingness to take accountability. In addition, ISO 26000 takes one step further and describes social responsibility as follows.

> Social responsibility involves an understanding of the broader expectations of society. A fundamental principle of social responsibility is respect for the rule of law and compliance with legally binding obligations. Social responsibility, however, also entails actions beyond legal compliance and the recognition of obligations to others that are not legally binding. These obligations arise out of widely shared ethical and other values (ISO26000, Section 3.3.2).

The first part of the discussion above explores statutory responsibility, which, in the context of this book, implies accountability, as the scope of compliance is clearly defined. Meanwhile, the latter part—'recognition of obligations to others that are not legally binding'—refers to what is not written in the law; thus, it is similar to infinite responsibility, whose scope cannot be limited in advance. We argue that responsibility is a spontaneous and subjective concept, which means that we should undertake it spontaneously and subjectively for some obligation. Although we may not be able to define it explicitly, we should not question the obligations associated with such responsibility but instead, judge voluntarily how to fulfil them.

In this way, ISO26000 addresses social responsibility that reflects the original concept of infinite responsibility. However, as for how to realise responsibility within an organisation, this standard requests organisation to assign and manage both accountability and responsibility at the appropriate hierarchical level in the organisation.

> Social responsibility should be an integral part of core organizational strategy with assigned responsibility and accountability at all appropriate levels of the organization. It should be reflected in decision making and considered in implementing activities (ISO26000, Section 3.3.4).

As discussed above, it becomes clear that in ISO 26000, there is an understanding that responsibility, as the same with accountability, can be assigned to each organisational level. Clearly, it is basic in management that assign accountability and responsibility respectively and manage those to whom they are assigned, with the understanding of accountability as the *obligation to explain* and responsibility as the *obligation to act*. Operating CSR in this way will be effective in solving some specific problems such as environmental destruction and human rights violations. However, is it possible that infinite responsibility (in which the scope is not limited) can be actually assigned in this way?[3] In spite of this difficulty, aside from ISO 26000, the approach of assigning such a responsibility is common in many CSR standards and guidelines, including the GRI standards.

---

[3] However, it is not unreasonable to assign infinite responsibility. Hirohide Takikawa relies on Robert Goodin's theory of general duty that is close to infinite responsibility, and discusses the concept of 'assigned responsibility'. In that case, the range of assigned responsibility can be understood as still being infinite. However, once responsibility is assigned, it is very difficult to dismiss the understanding that the scope is finite. This book aims to overcome this idea. Takikawa, H. (2020) Drawing national boundaries for global governance, in Takikawa, H. (ed.) *The Rule of Law and Democracy*, Franz Steiner Verlag, pp. 59–70.

ISO 26000 gathered the wisdom of CSR at that time and thus, it also included somehow the significance of infinite responsibility. However, when it comes to practical operations, it is driven by the idea of 'finite responsibility'. ISO 26000 introduces the idea of applying such a concept of responsibility to social and environmental issues to tackle these issues, but this alone may limit responsibility to merely accountability, which will contribute to the expansion of accountability. The question is how can this become a problem? We will consider this issue in relation to risk in the next section.

2.3 Expanded Accountability and Accumulated Risks

The responsibility to be fulfilled by a company is inevitably defined as accountability, which is then divided and assigned to the people in charge. However, it must be understood that not all problems would be solved by only expanding accountability, which can even be counterproductive in some cases.

This problem can be better understood from the perspective of risk. In modern society, a lot of risks that are rarely ever seen in human history have arisen due to the expansion and sophistication of the industrial society. For example, there would be no accident without means of transportation like aeroplanes, railroads, and automobiles, and no risk of collapse if there were no buildings, either high-rise or underground. Indeed, development in civilisation brings about risks that previously did not exist. Nuclear power is probably the biggest risk ever. In addition, during the financial crisis of 2007–2008 we experienced this with the global expansion of financial markets, resulting in enormous amounts of assets disappearing in a financial crash.

Many of these measures taken against such risks are to increase responsibility of those involved. Unclear responsibility has been defined explicitly, accountability has been set, and regulations including penalty and compensation have been developed so far. In the case of corporate scandals, clarification of unclear responsibility and new appointments of responsible people are often taken as the first measures. The responsibility of financial institutions and manufacturers are increasingly elaborated and getting stricter. Similarly, the responsibility of professionals, such as doctors and accountants, is becoming much heavier than before. Have you ever been given an unreadable number of financial contracts that are replete with details of the associated responsibilities? This is an example of expanding accountability in modern society.

Unfortunately, this does not guarantee that all risks can be avoided. No matter how finely the definable and divisible responsibilities are allocated, risks that cannot be controlled will continue to exist. We have already experienced how these uncontrolled risks could lead to catastrophes, including the accident at the Fukushima nuclear power plant. However, to address such problems, even though responsibilities are more judiciously allocated, and sanctions are strengthened in the event of inadequate fulfilment, people continue struggling to limit their responsibility as much as possible. This is a legitimate defensive response. If this happens, they will lose a wider perspective and the desire to see the whole beyond their own responsibility. This would accumulate risks that they cannot control.

There would be no problem if all risks could be defined and assigned; however, there exist, obviously, unidentifiable and unassignable risks due to the limitation of human perception. To identify and manage such risks, the idea of assigning responsibility is not sufficient. On the contrary, focusing on the assignable responsibility could impair one's ability to address unseen risks and thereby increase the overall risk. The accumulated risks will then all of a sudden turn into man-made disasters.

This holds true for environmental and social issues. Environmental destruction and human rights violations were not previously considered risks for companies, but how should management deal with such problems without taking them as a corporate responsibility? It is evident from our experience that, as with financial responsibility, defining the scope and assigning responsibility to relevant people cannot resolve these issues. Definitely, the assignment of responsibility is one of the important measures, but it would not be enough. However, given the range of issues, such as environmental conservation and human rights, emergent approaches that make all human beings think of what they can do spontaneously and that involve diverse people would be imperative.

There is limitation in trying to solve all problems solely by strengthening risk management. It is impossible to address risks that cannot be defined without introducing infinite responsibility in addition to finite and allocable responsibility. The key is how to manage infinite responsibility in a company. While this is an issue that is considered throughout this book, in the next section, we will discuss it from a human perspective.

2.4 Responsibility and Restoration of Wholeness

Implementing infinite responsibility leads to the restoration of human beings' wholeness. Human beings are born to be complete living creatures; nature has designed us in a way that we can fully use our abilities to conduct our daily lives. This is the same for work, and people are supposed to enjoy the pleasure of achieving a target by creating a single complete product whether in agriculture or industry.

However, with companies evolving into large organisations and the activities becoming more sophisticated and complicated, the tasks that an individual can do are naturally limited, making it more efficient to divide the work. Therefore, the work assigned to a person working for a modern enterprise is only a small part of the whole, and the inherent nature of people's wholeness is significantly impaired at work. Karl Marx criticised the problem as *alienation*, but the type of socialism he envisioned did not solve this problem.

Frederick Laloux regards this restoration of the wholeness of human beings as a critical issue in corporate management, and he has been exploring new forms of organisation. As a management consultant working with several companies,

Laloux divides the development of management into five stages and named the most advanced stage as a 'teal organisation'.

Laloux assumes that wholeness is based on the spirituality of human beings, which is a concept that is close to the idea of one's self being as it is. Self is the union of various elements, and it is also a part of the whole universe. Such ideas are the basis of wholeness and people will crave for wholeness when it is lost. In particular, in an efficient organisation, such as a corporate organisation that presupposes the division of labour, this deviation is becoming significant as Laloux states as follows.

> This longing for wholeness is at odd with the separation that most existing workplaces foster, albeit unconsciously-overemphasizing the ego and the rational while negating the spiritual and emotional; separating people based on the departments they work in, their rank, background, or level of performance; separating the professional from the personal; separating the organisation from its competitors and the ecosystem it is embedded in.[4]

In other words, Laloux points out that the work in a hierarchical organisation that presupposes division of labour has impaired the wholeness that human beings originally possessed. However, most business management has taken the enhancement of efficiency through division of labour so naturally that they overlook such impairment, and even the employees have not noticed it. Nevertheless, when they consider their own lives and the purpose of life, they might find that the price of giving up the wholeness of human beings in exchange for financial rewards is too enormous.

Laloux calls an organisation where employees can restore their wholeness and evolve to the stage of self-management as a teal organisation, where the concepts of responsibility and accountability are also important. By studying many cases of teal organisations, Laloux defined responsibility and accountability for a teal organisation as follows.

Responsibility and accountability

- We each have full responsibility for the organization. If we sense that something needs to happen, we have a duty to address it. It is not acceptable to limit our concern to the remit of our roles.
- Everyone must be comfortable with holding others accountable to their commitments through feedback and respectful confrontation.[5]

This concept of Laloux's responsibility leads to infinite responsibility. In a hierarchical organisation, an individual's 'responsibility' is limited to his/her assigned responsibilities and he/she is accountable for them. Conversely, assigning 'responsibility' with accountability forms a hierarchical organisation. It fosters an explicit, as well as implicit, rule not only that people will be punished if they do not discharge their own 'responsibility', but also that people will refrain from commenting on others' 'responsibility'. By contrast, the responsibility of an individual in a teal organisation is not limited but recognised as being for the whole organisation. Regarding accountability, rather than the vertical communication from the people who provide authority

---

[4] Laloux, F. (2014) *Reinventing Organizations: A Guide to Creating Organizations Inspired by the Next Stage of Human Consciousness*, Nelson Parker, p. 48.

[5] *Ibid.*, p. 231.

to those who are given this authority, horizontal accountability, which people share at the same level, has been recommended.

Laloux surveys companies that practise self-management and discusses in detail what are necessary to evolve to a teal organisation. Although we cannot fully explain his arguments here, we can say that it may not be impossible for a small company to change the whole organisational structure to become a teal organisation. However, it is quite difficult to transform a big hierarchical company that always pursues efficiency maximisation to become a teal organisation.

Nevertheless, even if it is impossible to modify the whole, the situation can be greatly improved by providing places where infinite responsibility can function in the organisation. Accountability as finite responsibility and infinite responsibility are not conflicting but compatible concepts. If we can provide spaces and projects based on infinite responsibility even in an organisation based on accountability, it will be meaningful for corporate management as well as those who work there, and thus for the whole society. This is the aim of emergent responsible management.

2.5 CSR as Infinite Responsibility

From the discussion so far, it can be understood that CSR should be based on infinite responsibility. Since CSR is literally the responsibility of a company to society, its contents should not be decided by the company but should be originally determined by society. However, since society is only an abstract concept, it cannot assign responsibility to companies. As the same with environmental issues, which are one of the biggest social concerns, the natural environment cannot speak, nor can it directly demand for human responsibility.

Therefore, companies must seek their own responsibility for society and the environment by themselves. The scope of their responsibility is not predetermined. Of course, many corporate social and environmental responsibilities are given externally in the form of laws, standards, or targets. However, many of them are regarded as finite responsibilities, and companies need to take accountability, but it does not mean that this is all about CSR.

What kinds of problems in society should be solved? What kind of society do we want it to be? What kind of contributions can we make for society? The collection of such thoughts from different people forms the concept of social responsibility. Only quite a small part of it is written in the laws, guidelines, and standards because people's daily life will be impaired if they are violated. However, the original responsibility is infinite. CSR is essentially supposed to be an act of exploring this kind of responsibility; otherwise, it is not different from the normal compliance with the rules.

However, undoubtedly practising CSR as a corporate activity at a level of infinite responsibility is very difficult under a hierarchical organisation. It is difficult to deal with matters such as compliance with the concept of infinite responsibility alone.

Therefore, there is a need for a system that combines both activities based on infinite responsibility and finite accountability. However, even if we can conceptually separate infinite responsibility and finite accountability, combining them in the same activity is likely to end up in transforming infinite responsibility into finite accountability. For this reason, we believe that one of the effective ways to deal with it is to launch a new project that is based on infinite responsibility, independent of other corporate activities.

Emergent responsible management is a new concept for it. It is beyond the scope of conventional CSR and is tended to cover the entire corporate management. CSR has been originally a concept for such intention, however, when abbreviated as 'CSR' along with the issuance of many guidelines and policy documents, companies began to establish CSR departments in response, and its role becomes fixed gradually. Infinite responsibility is essentially a concept that overcomes such limitations; thus, it is necessary to be free from the stereotype of CSR. If the responsibility to be sought is infinite, the action of seeking the responsibility must be voluntary rather than mandatory, and it necessarily emerges due to the involvement of others. In the next chapter, we will discuss this issue of emergence.

Chapter 3
Transforming to Emergent Responsible Management

Katsuhiko Kokubu

Abstract The purpose of this chapter is to shed light on the notion of emergence as one of the essential elements that underpins the theory of emergent responsible management. When discussing responsibility in corporate management, it is important to understand the spontaneity and activeness of human beings, as well as the emergence brought about by practice. Since emergent responsible management is an emergent practice that occurs between oneself and others, promoting such practice in an organisation requires some specific measures, including the establishment of corporate philosophy and involvement of others. Although it is difficult to promote infinite responsibility in a hierarchical organisation based on accountability, to resolve social issues such as the SDGs, implementing emergent responsible management as a project could be one of the solutions to over come the limitation of organisational hierarchy.

3.1 Emergence and Responsibility

In the previous chapters, we have discussed that responsibility is essentially subjective and rooted in the inner part of human beings since it is others who approach the self; the corresponding practice, as a result, is inherently emergent.The term *emergence* was originally used in natural science, and Pier Luigi Luisi, a molecular biologist, describes the notion of emergence as 'the onset of novel properties that arise when a higher level of complexity is formed from components of lower complexity, where these properties are not present'.[1] In the world of biology, as Luisi reveals, the concept of emergence connotes an opportunity for self-organisation, and the direction of self-organisation cannot be programmed in advance.

This concept of emergence has been used often in management studies as well, capturing the interaction between agents and the generated value in the context of knowledge creation and innovation. For example, Jiro Kokuryo, who adopts the

[1] Luisi, P. L. (2006) *The Emergence of Life: From Chemical Origins to Biology*, Cambridge University Press, p. 112.

K. Kokubu et al., *Emergent Responsible Management*, Kobe University Monograph Series in Social Science Research, https://doi.org/10.1007/978-981-19-0416-5_3

concept of emergence to the field of management to develop a theory, claims that emergent value creation is a situation where 'a lot of players are working without necessarily assuming specific consequences in advance; in the meantime, a variety of resources will be combined and new and unexpected values are generated one after another'.[2] It is important to note the existence of multiple players and unexpected results.

Amid the changing business environment, it is increasingly difficult to manage a company solely through 20th-century-type organisational operations that focus on internal management control. It is also required to maintain and manage various connections with external entities beyond the organisation, such as management of interfaces with customers and open architectures. The concept of *emergent management* proposed by Kokuryo can be understood as a concept to adapt to such changes in the business environment. Emergent management emphasises the way to construct the organisation process and platform that generates some type of emergence in the organisation, which is in common with emergent responsible management.

Emergent responsible management is not a top-down management approach; rather, it is carried out through a spontaneous exploration of social issues by employees who work on-site, as well as by repeatedly interacting with both internal and external stakeholders. As a result, unexpected values can be created for society. Since responsibility is a concept based on responsiveness to others, it is essentially a subjective and spontaneous action that is likely to generate something unexpected for both sides. Emergent practices, unlike objective accountability, cannot be managed by contracts, rules, targets and the like. Therefore, the same with self-organisation, it is necessary for management to design appropriate systems and mechanisms that support such practice.

Henry Mintzberg, a prominent business scholar in the United States, proposed the concept of *emergent strategy*, emphasising the importance of emergence on strategy formulation. Management strategies cannot be fully developed with only planning; some strategies are gradually formed even without being noticed. According to Mintzberg, planning and emergent strategies are at two extremes of a line.[3]

As the emergent responsible management advocated in this book involves all employees as executors, it is different from the strategy formulation by the management, but there are some commonalities between the two. Emergent practices are at the opposite end of general management methods such as the PDCA cycle. However, it is important to recognise that they are not contradictory but just at the extreme ends of the same line. Mintzberg points out that crafting is necessary to integrate the two extremes. This thought is also applicable in emergent responsible management.

---

[2] Kokuryo, J. and Platform Design Lab (2011) *Emergent Management Platform: Creating an Information Infrastructure for Collaboration*, Nikkei Publishing Inc., p. 2 (in Japanese). This definition by Kokuryo is discussed in detail in Chap. 9.

[3] Mintzberg, H. (1987) Crafting Strategy. *Harvard Business Review*, Vol. 65, pp. 66–75.

Before considering the details of emergent responsible management, based on our recent survey, we would like to take a look at the recent trends of CSR activities in Japan regarding the values towards CSR, the role of employees, the leadership of top management, and so on.

3.2 CSR of Japanese Companies

We conducted a questionnaire survey on CSR with 1,413 companies listed[4] in the CSR Corporate Directory (Toyo Keizai) in November 2018 and received 171 valid respondents. All questions were asked on a seven-point Likert scale, with 7 point denoting 'exactly like that' and 1 point, denoting 'totally different'. We pick up some related topics from this survey to show the trends of CSR in Japan.

First, we asked about the respondents' values related to CSR. The guidelines for individuals to consider responsibility should ideally be based on social norms and ethics. However, when considering a corporate organisation, the standards are often established based on the corporate philosophy. As such, we asked whether corporate philosophy was the basis of CSR. As shown in Fig. 3.1, the highest score was

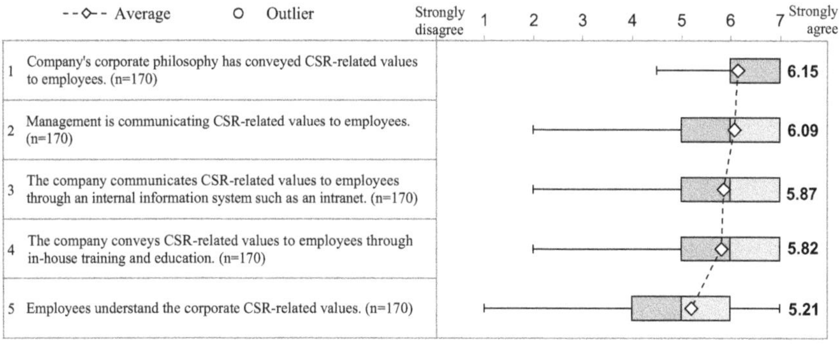

Fig. 3.1 Values for CSR[5]

[4] This survey is from a joint research with Jaehong Kim at Kanto Gakuen University.

[5] The table is called a 'box plot' and shows the variation of data. ◇ is the average value, and the range of the minimum and maximum values of an answer is indicated by a line, from the first quarter point (25% of the total number of answers) to the third quarter-point (75% of the whole). The box is divided into two parts by the median.

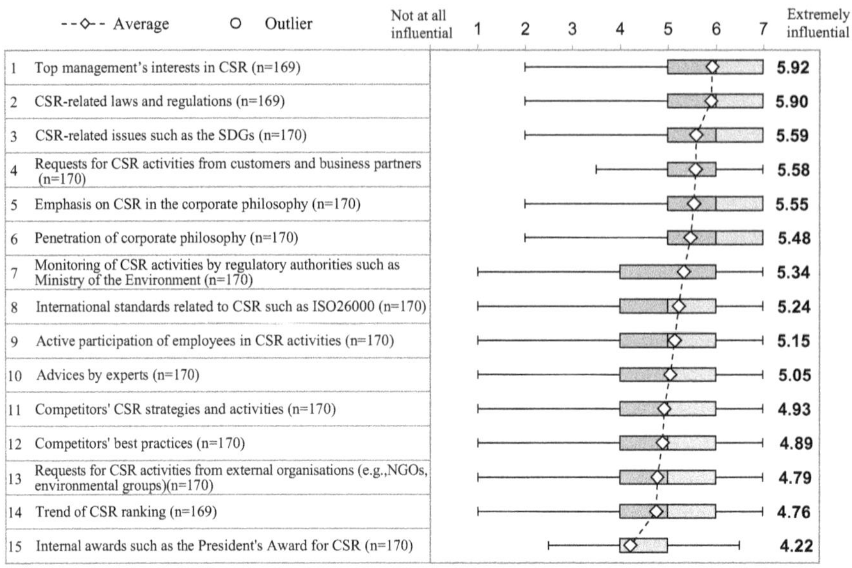

Fig. 3.2 Factors affecting CSR activities

given to the statement 'Company's corporate philosophy has conveyed CSR-related values to employees' (average 6.15), followed by 'Management is communicating CSR-related values to employees' (average 6.09). For many companies, the corporate philosophy reflects CSR, and top management has tried to communicate it to employees.

However, with regard to factors that affect CSR activities (Fig. 3.2), the most influential factors were 'Top management's interests in CSR' (5.92) and 'CSR-related laws and regulations' (5.90), with 'Emphasis on CSR in the corporate philosophy' ranking fifth (5.55). 'Active participation of employees in CSR activities' (5.15) ranked ninth, lower than the influences of customers, business partners, and regulators. These results imply that when conducting CSR activities, although Japanese companies have recognised the importance of corporate philosophy, the influence of laws and regulations tends to be greater. Moreover, the participation of employees is emphasised with the average score of over 5 points, but they are not considered as the most influential stakeholders.

Furthermore, as for the top management's leadership regarding employees' involvement in CSR, as shown in Fig. 3.3, 'Top management requires employees to comply with CSR policy and guidelines' (5.74) ranked first, followed by 'Top

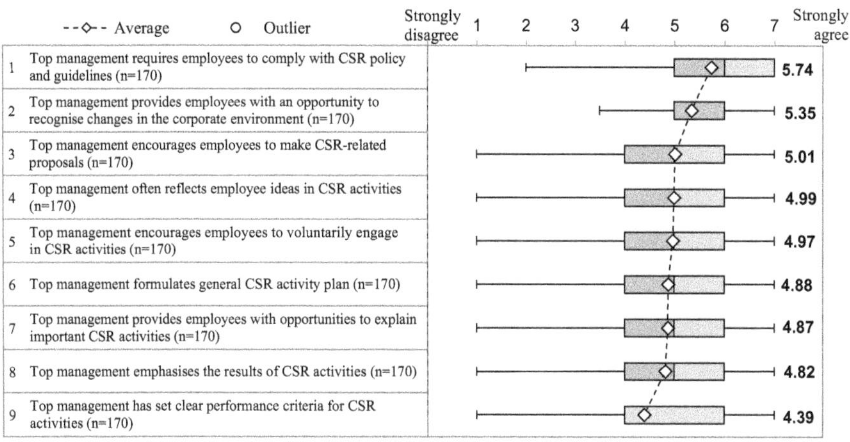

Fig. 3.3 Leadership of top management in CSR

management provides employees with an opportunity to recognise changes in the corporate environment' (5.35), 'Top management encourages employees to make CSR-related proposals' (5.01), 'Top management often reflects employee ideas in CSR activities' (4.99), and 'Top management encourages employees to voluntarily engage in CSR activities' (4.97). In comparison, 'Top management has set clear performance criteria for CSR activities' (4.39) ranked low. These results show that the top management often promotes employees' voluntary behaviour, although the performance standards are not sufficiently developed for CSR activities.

These results have only partly described the CSR activities of Japanese companies and further analysis is needed for generalisation. Nevertheless, it has shown the importance of corporate philosophy and the role of employees in CSR. However, it is clear that CSR is greatly affected by laws and regulations, and that the top management emphasises compliance with them more than voluntary actions. This indicates that responsibility and accountability, based on our definition, are mixed in CSR practice. Therefore, to envision emergent responsible management, it is desirable to approach this topic from a more comprehensive perspective, and take the entire corporate management into account, in addition to the existing CSR activities. The key points are the corporate philosophy, employees, and social issues. We explore these three points as follows.

3.3 Corporate Philosophy as the Starting Point of Emergent Responsible Management

Those who want to start a company must first have some broad mission. Only a few companies are set up simply for money, which would not survive for long since they are not able to sustain support from society. A company is organised to meet some social needs, and profits are a necessary resource for its continuation, which is commonly understood by founders of companies.

However, with time going on and more people working for the company since its establishment, there is a danger that it is difficult to keep the founder's principles perpetuated, in which case, the company is likely to take a different direction from where it started. Therefore, the corporate philosophy is disseminated to remind employees about the founder's principles. The corporate philosophy describes why the company exists in society, and is expressed simply in a way that is easy for employees to remember but does not specify the detailed activities conducted daily.

The corporate philosophy is usually abstract as it represents the shared spirit needed in carrying out daily work within the company. Being abstract means a commonality among concrete objects, thus it can be more widely applied. That is why most of the famous corporate philosophies are abstract. For example, Panasonic's corporate philosophy was defined by its founder Konosuke Matsushita in 1929: 'We will devote ourselves to the progress and development of society and the well-being of people through our business activities, thereby enhancing the quality, of life throughout the world'.

The *Five Main Principles of Toyoda* are a written statement of the teaching of Sakichi Toyoda, the founder of Toyota. The principles were first released in 1935, the fifth anniversary of Sakichi's death.

- Always be faithful to your duties, thereby contributing to the Company and to the overall good.
- Always be studious and creative, striving to stay ahead of the times.
- Always be practical and avoid frivolousness.
- Always strive to build a homelike atmosphere at work that is warm and friendly.
- Always have respect for spiritual matters, and remember to be grateful at all times.

Although traditional Japanese words are used, none of them defines specific actions, but only indicate directions when taking action. Other examples of modern corporate philosophy are SoftBank's corporate philosophy—'Information Revolution-Happiness for everyone'—and the Rakuten Group's corporate philosophy—'contributing to society by creating value through innovation and entrepreneurship'.

Such corporate philosophies are abstract, even though the words used have changed over time. However, being defined in an abstract way, the corporate philosophy aims to encourage employees to take some action. For example, as with SoftBank's 'Information Revolution-Happiness for everyone', employees are encouraged to take action for the 'happiness for everyone'. The same goes for the corporate philosophy of Panasonic, Toyota, and Rakuten.

The corporate philosophy is meaningless if it is just recorded as empty sentences and not linked to actions. However, if it can be linked to action, then it is possible to change people's behaviour in the company to adapt to the change of the environment. This would enable the corporate philosophy to survive over time. Therefore, to make the corporate philosophy meaningful, it is necessary to have a mechanism that links it with corporate actions.

Moreover, if you look at some of the corporate philosophies, you will notice that most companies emphasise their contribution to society. This is natural since companies are founded to address social issues as we discussed before, yet it can easily be changed to the pursuit of economic goals over time. Certainly, without economic profits, a company cannot survive in a society, but if it only pursues profit, it is meaningless for the company to exist in a society. It is the corporate philosophy that reminds all of this to everyone in a company. Therefore, we believe that the basis for emergent responsible management can be found in the corporate philosophy.

Furthermore, it should be noted that since the corporate philosophy is abstract, the actions taken to realise it must be essentially spontaneous, and the corresponding practice will emerge through the interactions among various stakeholders. In other words, to realise the corporate philosophy, there is no predetermined purpose, and it is required that employees should think and act by themselves. Such practice extends beyond the original intention, making it an emergent practice.

3.4 Employee as Leader of Activities

As responsibility is based on responding to the call of others, it is not confined to oneself but always involves others. In the case of a company, others refer to those who are outside the organisation. Therefore, companies are required to search for responsibilities that exist outside. External stakeholders may make some requests to the company, but that does not include all the responsibilities. Rather, most responsibilities cannot be expressed with a certain voice, just as a baby cannot make demands with its own words. If the management, as only part of the employees, is supposed to search for the targets of such practices, emergent responsible management would be out of reach. Each and every employee is required to search for his/her own responsibility.

Responsibility, as the philosopher André Comte-Sponville points out, cannot be taken by an organisation such as a company, but can only be borne by people. Furthermore, responsibility cannot be delegated to others[6] either. In emergent responsible management, the problem is how to address such responsibility in corporate activities. The corporate philosophy is regarded as one way to consider it, but it is not enough. It is necessary to make employees aware of their individual responsibilities and get involved in the practice. The specific mechanisms and activities will be

[6] Comte-Sponville, A. (2006) *El capitalismo es moral (Is Capitalism Mortal?)*, Kinokuniya Bookstore (Japanese version).

discussed in the next chapter, along with an examination of company cases. Here, we highlight the importance of the role of employees.

For a company, the people it hires are not only employees but are citizens as well. The difference is that being a citizen is more fundamental in the sense that employees can quit the company at any time, but it is nearly impossible for them to choose not to be citizens. Employees are both internal and external (as citizens) to a company. Therefore, it is essential that a company, as an organisation, responds to the social responsibility recognised by employees as citizens. This is why we must stimulate employees' spontaneity in emergent responsible management.

Moreover, among citizens, employees are the most concerned stakeholders of the company. In the area of CSR, many guidelines, such as ISO26000, strongly value the opinions of stakeholders; thus, activities such as stakeholder engagement are frequently conducted. However, general concerns from society regarding a certain company are not always significant. A common problem for those in charge of CSR reports is that there are no readers despite their efforts to prepare it. However, employees who work for a company are very interested in the company. Encouraging them to view the company as a citizen, rather than as an employee, would provide them with a better understanding of corporate social responsibility. Then, if linked to actions, emergent responsible management would be activated.

More importantly, we highlight that the fulfilment of responsibility creates social connections. The philosopher Iris Marion Young advocates a *social connection model* of responsibility.[7] She argues that concerning structural injustices, such as inequality and environmental destruction, rather than the responsibility being pursued by a particular individual, these issues must be resolved in a social context where the responsibility is connected. Based on her model, responsibility essentially occurs in social connections. Thus, fulfilling responsibility means creating new connections. If people aim to solve social issues, it will inevitably create new connections and networks in society. Therefore, emergent responsible management can be recognised as a *social connection model of management*.

To carry out emergent responsible management, it is necessary to respect the inherent perspective of participating employees as citizens and to release them as much as possible from the organisational hierarchy. To solve social issues, if a project—wherein members seek to act with awareness of their own responsibility—is developed as an organisational action, this may conflict with the accountability assigned within the company. Ideally, emergent responsible management projects should free the participants from their hierarchical positions in the company so that they can address the issue on an equal footing, and thereby make emergent effects more prominent.

---

[7] Young, I. M. (2014) *Responsibility for Justice*, Oxford University Press.

3.5 Addressing Social Issues: SDGs Initiatives

How should we find social issues to address? This requires effort to connect a company's capabilities and resources with corresponding social issues. It is easier to be inspired by social issues that have already been recognised globally or locally. That is why the SDGs adopted by the United Nations in 2015 are supposed to work as a useful guide. The SDGs consist of 17 goals and 169 targets that must be achieved worldwide by 2030, and efforts from private organisations are also acknowledged. Since the SDGs are globally approved goals, it makes sense to adopt them as a guide to explore social issues. The SDGs are receiving much attention worldwide, and many companies' CSR reports are published with the logos of the 17 goals. However, in fact, it only shows the relationship between the business and the 17 goals, and in many cases, it is not clear how companies will address the issues as a commitment to SDGs.

If companies try to work on the SDGs, it is necessary to shift from the conventional *inside-out* approach to an *outside-in* approach, as emphasised by the introductory guide *SDG Compass.*[8] The inside-out approach is to make a commitment externally based on targets constructed internally. This is based on the company's existing capabilities; thus, many of the current CSR activities can be categorised as an inside-out approach. In comparison, with the *outside-in* approach, the goals to be fulfilled by a company are determined externally instead of internally, and how companies should react to it should be questioned. Since the SDGs are goals to be achieved by 2030, companies must deal with them in an outside-in approach.

This outside-in approach is common with infinite responsibility, as it also requires responding to others. Therefore, if a company is committed to achieving the SDGs, it is necessary to take on the challenge in an outside-in approach. Thus, if companies address specific issues such as the SDGs, they need to know that the responsibility they are taking is different from the day-to-day operations of their business. In general, if profitability is too low to reach a certain level, managers should consider withdrawing from such an operation. However, if they are working on the SDGs, they should make decisions with a longer-term perspective instead of simply for short-term returns. Thus, it is necessary to make a clear commitment to the goals set in an outside-in approach.

It is the same when considering other social issues aside from the SDGs. Commencing with any issue based on emergent responsible management means acting with awareness of the responsibility that goes beyond the scope of general business; no difference between emergent responsible management and conventional management will be seen if there is no such understanding.

---

[8] The SDG Compass is a practical guideline for companies working on the SDGs, jointly published by the GRI, the United Nations Global Compact, and the WBCSD in 2016. This is discussed in detail in Chap. 11.

3.6 Organisations for Emergent Responsible Management

The concept of emergent responsible management is similar to an innovative organisational paradigm called a *teal organisation* or *holacracy system*. The teal organisation advocated by Frederick Laloux is based on self-management by employees and requires everyone to be fully responsible for the whole organisation, as described in Chap. 2.[9] Holacracy is a new organisational management method (advocated by Brian J. Robertson) that eliminates layers within an organisation, empowers all members, and organises the work instead of the people. It is a mechanism where employees have the responsibility and the authority to deal with tensions.[10]

The teal organisation and the holacracy system define the concept of responsibility in a way that is similar to infinite responsibility, which is against conventional management that assigns finite accountability and authorities to individuals to shape the organisation. Both paradigms aim to create a flat, spontaneous and emergent organisation that focuses on how to organise work systematically under the premise that everyone is responsible for everything. This is the basic way of thinking when designing an organisation based on infinite responsibility.

Therefore, if emergent responsible management is to be applied to the whole corporate management system, a teal organisation or holacracy system might be needed as a new management model. This is the organisational form that is inevitably required when pursuing infinite responsibility. However, for most companies that already have been organised by allocating authorities with accountabilities, it is almost impossible to transform the organisational structure completely into a teal or holacracy type of organisation. It is difficult to imagine that a large company that currently designed as a hierarchical organisation will be replaced by a teal organisation or a holacracy system in the near future.

However, to resolve social issues such as the SDGs or restore the wholeness of human beings as Laloux points out, it is necessary to promote infinite responsibility within an organisation. It is difficult to implement this in a hierarchical organisation based on accountability. As one of the solutions, companies could adopt emergent responsible management as a project, and within its scope, they can create a flat and emergent site by overcoming the limitation of the organisational hierarchy. In this way, we are not only able to pursue infinite responsibility but also bring innovation by questioning the existing way of thinking based on accountability. Therefore, in this book we are not arguing for the perfect reorganisation of a company towards emergent responsible management; instead, we want to find a way to work on it by engaging in emergent responsible management projects.

In the following chapters, we provide five examples of companies to elaborate the concept of emergent responsible management. Each case is introduced with one project or several activities involving different projects; thus, the discussions are

[9] Laloux, F. (2014) *Reinventing Organizations: A Guide to Creating Organizations Inspired by the Next Stage of Human Consciousness*, Nelson Parker.

[10] Robertson, B. J. (2015) *Holacracy: The New Management System for a Rapidly Changing World*, Henry Holt and Co.

limited to only some parts of the whole company's operations. These companies are probably not explicitly conscious of infinite responsibility, so they might not be the perfect examples of emergent responsible management. However, there is certainly something in these activities beyond the scope of the traditional framework of corporate management, and we would like to refine it to develop a prototype for emergent responsible management.

Chapter 4
OMRON: Realising the Corporate Philosophy Driven Projects

Katsuhiko Kokubu and Kimitaka Nishitani

Abstract Emergent responsible management has already been practised by certain companies; thus, it is not simply a utopian dream. This chapter and following four chapters aim to provide examples by examining how activities reflecting its fundamental elements have been practised in those companies. This chapter analyses the experience of OMRON, a major electronics manufacturer by investigating its Corporate Philosophy Driven Projects, which aims to practice the corporate philosophy. One mechanism for this purpose is 'The OMRON Global Awards' (TOGA). Under this award scheme, various projects have been launched by employees worldwide to foster a corporate culture that realises the OMRON Principle through their business. OMRON's corporate-philosophy-driven projects are not narrowly defined CSR activities but rather, are initiatives based on its corporate philosophy of 'creating a better society' and the value of creating social needs by solving social issues. These projects are typical examples of emergent responsible management as employees are directed to targets that cannot be determined in advance and that create social value for stakeholders.

4.1 OMRON's Initiatives

OMRON, founded in 1933 by Kazuma Tateishi, is a major electronics manufacturer that mainly provides control devices and electronic components. The founder's eldest son, Takao, and his third son, Yoshio, took over the business from him, and in 2003, Hisao Sakuta was appointed as the first president that is not from the Tateishi family. Since 2011, Yoshihito Yamada, appointed by the President Nomination Advisory Committee, has been the president. As a member of the Tateishi family, Fumio, the founder's fifth son, has been appointed as the Chairman of the Board.

With 'Sensing & Control + Think' as its core technology, OMRON is engaged in the control equipment, healthcare, in-vehicle, social systems, and electronic components businesses, achieving sales of approximately 860 billion yen in the fiscal year ending March 2018. The spirit of OMRON's founder, Kazuma Tateishi, has been handed down to the present generation. In 1959, OMRON's corporate philosophy entitled 'Our Mission' was summarised as 'To improve lives and contribute to a

K. Kokubu et al., *Emergent Responsible Management*, Kobe University Monograph Series in Social Science Research, https://doi.org/10.1007/978-981-19-0416-5_4

better society', which reflects Kazuma's life lesson: 'Those who are best in making people happy are the happiest'.

OMRON has inherited the philosophy that 'Business should create value for society through its key practices' and has been enthusiastically engaging in CSR activities ahead of other companies. In 2004, they changed their corporate report from 'Environmental Report' to 'Corporate Public Entity Report' and started to emphasise the social role of the company. In 2012, OMRON published its first 'Integrated Report'[1] and has always led the CSR of Japanese companies.

OMRON's corporate management is based on the corporate philosophy. OMRON developed its corporate philosophy systematically in 1990 and revised it three times to adapt to the trend of the time. Now, they call it the 'OMRON Principle'. Since the company's purpose is to 'contribute to a better society', CSR should be embedded into its corporate management. However, what exactly is 'a better society'? Kazuma's philosophy did not provide any specific content either. Therefore, both management and employees must constantly explore what 'a better society' should be.

This exploration does not necessarily lead to actions simply by reciting the corporate philosophy. OMRON has fostered employees' understanding and realisation of the corporate philosophy by encouraging them to put OMRON's principles into practice, and as a result, succeeded in disseminating the corporate philosophy. These activities are not limited to CSR, but aim to solve social issues through corporate activities, which can be a model for emergent responsible management. In the following section, we will discuss these activities inspired by OMRON's principles from the perspective of emergent responsible management.

4.2 Corporate Philosophy and TOGA

As stated earlier, Omron's corporate philosophy entitled 'Our Mission' is 'To improve lives and contribute to a better society', which was enacted in 1959. Under this mission, 'Our Values' has the following points.

- **Innovation Driven by Social Needs**
- Be a pioneer in creating inspired solutions for the future.
- **Challenging Ourselves**
- Pursue new challenges with passion and courage.
- **Respect for all**
- Act with integrity and encourage everyone's potential.

OMRON's corporate philosophy has been reflected in its management since its foundation. Yoshihito Yamada has been devoted to further embedding the 'OMRON Principles' into the company's management since his appointment as president. Yamada formulated a 10-year long-term vision—'Value Generation (VG) 2020' with

[1] OMRON won the 'Sincere Company Award' at the 17th 'IR Excellent Company Award' hosted by the Japan IR Association in 2012.

the corporate philosophy at its core. In an interview, Yamada said that 'OMRON is a company with a corporate philosophy that strongly emphasises the public nature of a company, including "Creating a better society" and "Contributing to the development of society through business", that's why we declare "Generate Value = Create Value"'.[2]

The corporate philosophy did not stem from its business domains; instead, it is the corporate philosophy that creates business domains in OMRON. Yamada commented on this point, claiming that 'Since OMRON's management is based on its corporate philosophy, we do not limit our business domains or areas. Creating a better society is our principle, and business domains and areas can be different as long as the technology is in common'.[3] In other words, while business domains and areas expand in general, and the corporate philosophy works as a centripetal force when OMRON narrows down whether the domains and areas truly match its philosophy.

However, words are not enough to reflect the corporate philosophy in management, let alone to make people take action. Practice is needed to convert words into reality. Since his appointment as the president, Yamada has continuously devoted himself to the practice of the corporate philosophy. One mechanism proposed for this purpose is 'The OMRON Global Awards' (TOGA). It is an award scheme for employees worldwide to foster a corporate culture that realises the 'OMRON Principle' through their business. TOGA has three key features, namely, (1) entrants are required to declare and work in teams; (2) the criteria for evaluation are based on the efforts to conform to the 'OMRON Principles'; and (3) the theme of the activities should be shared with the whole company. The team consists of three or more people, and the activities through the whole year will be evaluated. TOGA is a voluntary activity of employees, and the team can be carried out within departments or cross-functionally and even can be expanded into a global activity.

TOGA started in FY2012, and the number of participants in the first year was 20,828 with 2,481 themes. The number of participants has been increasing every year, and in seven years (by FY2018), a total of 275,250 employees participated and worked on 31,000 themes. The annual schedule of TOGA is as follows: (1) from May to July, submission of application based on discussions in the workplace; (2) from December to January, sharing and evaluation of activities by the business unit or company; and (3) on May 10, the anniversary of the company's founding, a global award ceremony is held where the winners are commended by the president. At the TOGA global award ceremony in May 2018, a total of 13 'Gold Award' themes were selected—four in Japan, four in China, two in Asia, one in Europe, one in the United States, and one in Korea.

TOGA manages the cost of holding the global and regional competition and the award prize on a company-level budget, but the practical activities are all carried out through daily work; the management of the activities and the budget allocation are operated by the business unit. At first, TOGA was an event-oriented initiative, but since around 2015, the promotion via business units has been taking shape and

[2] *Diamond Quarterly*, Summer 2018, p. 7.

[3] *Ibid.*, p. 9.

TOGA has evolved into activities more closely related to a business since then. In the next section, we introduce some of OMRON's representative projects that have a particularly strong appeal for social issues.

4.3 Cases of Realising OMRON's Principles-Based Projects

4.3.1 A New Form Challenging the Common Sense of Recruitment and Job-Hunting for Small and Medium-Sized Enterprises

This project, led by Naoya Etani from Nagoya Branch of Omron Personnel (OPC, now Omron Expert Link), received the TOGA Gold Award in 2017. OPC, as a comprehensive human resource service company, is a subsidiary that is responsible for the recruitment and training of the OMRON Group. Besides, it also offers labour dispatch and recruitment service for other companies.

The project by Etani and his colleagues aimed to solve two problems: the needs of small and medium-sized enterprises (SMEs) and the problem of young people who have difficulties in finding jobs. The government has also recognised the necessity to support such young people, and the Ministry of Health, Labour, and Welfare in Japan has implemented the 'Youth Career Support Program' since FY2014. This program is a project in which a human resource service company certified by the Ministry provides employment support service for young people who have graduated but have no or little experience in finding jobs. OPC has participated as a private company since 2015 but in 2016, it only succeeded in helping three people hired as regular employees and was unable to break through.

In 2016, Etani and his colleagues realised that this project fits the purpose of TOGA and came up with the idea of working on it as a TOGA project. As mentioned above, TOGA is adopted to support the practice of OMRON's values, namely 'innovation driven by social needs', 'challenging ourselves' and 'respect for all'. Etani thinks that their project does not only match the social needs of 'inexperienced people who seek full-time employment' and 'SMEs who lack manpower', but it is also the result of deep consideration of the principle 'respect for all' as demonstrated by supporting young people who have difficulties in finding jobs.

To work on this issue as a TOGA project, Etani called on five members who agreed on its purpose, and in May 2016, a youth employment support project was launched as a TOGA project. First, they set the key performance indicator (KPI) of the number of full-time employments to 30 people, compared with three in the previous year. Although this project was developed from general business activities, Etani appreciated that working on it as a TOGA project made it easier to bring social value to the forefront as opposed to economic demands, thus making it more appealing internally. In addition, through the TOGA selection process from in-house competition to all of Japan, the attitude of colleagues who were initially reluctant about the project changed, and it was obvious that the number of 'fans' in the company increased.

One of the features of the project is that it reversed the conventional matching mechanism. Usually, it is the companies that set up the booths and the job seekers visit the booths, but Etani reversed the situation so that companies would go to the job seekers' booths instead. With this reversed mechanism, job seekers who have lost their self-confidence can now experience their own market value for the first time, and companies can discover the potential of young people (Fig. 4.1).

In the past, the recruitment follows the steps of application submission, job interview and finally an unofficial offer, but here again the order is reversed. Making the work experience the first step, job seekers can dispel any misgivings about the company, improving their success in finding a job. In this way, Etani and his colleagues named the new form of support that challenges the conventional wisdom and mechanisms of job-hunting for young people and recruitment of SMEs as 'de-normal', and this catchphrase also succeeded in increasing recognition. Consequently, the results were great in FY2016 compared with FY2015 as shown in Table 4.1.

By supporting young people who cannot find jobs, as well as SMEs who cannot secure human resources, Etani and his colleagues realised that the biggest reason for failing is treating the reason of failure as something that cannot be changed by

Fig. 4.1 Recruiter in a Company Going around the Job Seeker's Booth

Table 4.1 Comparison of the Results of Recruitment Support Activities

	Initial participants	People completed training	Dispatched employees	Full-time employees
2015	65	46	7	3
2016	103	83	39	31
In total	168	129	46	34

Source Internal documents in OMRON

oneself. They understood that it is important to challenge something that remains unchanged and take actions to change it as soon as possible. Furthermore, Etani explained that members who participated in this project were able to identify areas that needed changes by finding new tasks. This is exactly the case where initiatives by employees in the TOGA project created emergent practices.

4.3.2 Revitalise the Area with Renewable Energy! Commercialisation of Solar Power Generation Utilising Abandoned Cultivated Land in Miyazu City, Kyoto Prefecture

This project, led by Hirosuke Tomatsu and his colleagues from Omron Field Engineering (OFE), won the TOGA Silver Award in 2017. OFE is a subsidiary of Omron Social Solutions, Inc., a project of its Energy Management Business Unit (EM Business Unit).

This project was launched as the first project of the EM Business Division's business plan of 'Local production for local consumption business of renewable energy' in FY2014. Renewable energy, such as solar power, has become widespread in Japan, due to the effect of the Japanese government's policy. However, their original business model has raised concerns that it may result in big capitalists drawing profits from the region. Therefore, OFE decided to pursue a business model of 'local production for local consumption', in which the renewable energy projects contribute to local revitalisation. This background reflects the corporate philosophy of solving social issues and creating a better society.

Developing a solar power generation business in the region would contribute to the local economy, but if it could bring more to the local area, that would be even better. The project in Miyazu City was promoted against the background that the waste of abandoned cultivated land has become a major social problem. The project aimed to solve not only the supply of renewable energy but also other social problems. Even if the abandoned cultivated land can be prevented from being degraded, it does not generate any direct profits for OMRON. Therefore, it is a plan that may be questioned as a business activity, but its approval by the company can be seen as a reflection on the corporate philosophy.

Fig. 4.2 Abandoned Cultivated Land (Yura Area)

In cooperation with a local construction company, a special purpose company aiming for solar power was established to install solar panels on the abandoned cultivated land in the Yura area of Miyazu City. This project was developed to contribute to the local economy by revitalising the construction industry, increasing the flow of capital, creating additional tax revenues, and so on. However, securing abandoned cultivated land for a power station required the approval of the landowners, making it extremely difficult. It was a very difficult task to sign a lease with about 100 landowners because a large number of landowners had flown out of the area without lending or selling their land to others. With the cooperation of the local mayor and the chairman of the residents' association, Tomatsu recalled, 'We were able to achieve this with enthusiasm and a heart that never gives up' (Figs. 4.2 and 4.3).

OMRON's corporate philosophy has had a significant impact on this activity and it also helped in gaining the understanding from other companies when conducting business. In particular, local construction companies had no experience in such business before and were sceptical at first. It was OMRON's corporate philosophy that played a deciding role in gaining trust and turning this project into a success. Local companies were also deeply touched by OMRON's employees who kept frankly explaining their corporate philosophy. This is also a good example of how responsibility creates social connections.

This project was not designed to apply for TOGA, but it fully followed the same spirit, which reflected the corporate philosophy. As a result, Tomatsu and his colleagues said that receiving the Silver Award gave all employees a great sense of achievement and provided the driving force for developing similar projects throughout Japan.

Fig. 4.3 After Installation of Solar Panels

4.3.3 Human Resource Development to Live up to Our Principle

Last but not least, we would like to introduce an overseas case. This is a project from Mexico that won the Gold Award in 2017. This project is an initiative of OMRON Automotive Electronics Corporation's Mexico-based manufacturing office (OAX),[4] which is engaged in the automotive electrical components business. Guanajuato, Mexico, where this office is located, is Mexico's largest automobile manufacturing base, and many auto makers and related companies have been operating there (Fig. 4.4).

In such an environment, OAX used to suffer from a high turnover rate. In 2016, the monthly turnover rate was 6.25%, with 75% of full-time employees changing jobs annually. A high turnover rate does not only increase the cost of training for employees but also weakens loyalty to a company and destroys a feeling of unity as an organisation. To reduce the turnover rate, OAX turned to OMRON's corporate philosophy—'respect for all'—which is also the teaching of Kazuma Tateishi.

After analysing the causes of demission, OAX realised the need of project to attract employees to stay at the company. Inspired by the guiding principle, 'respect for all', they developed initiatives, including a 'human resource development project' to develop leaders, an 'on boarding project' to help new employees settle down more easily, and a 'social project' to understand their own social values. A thorough education program for unskilled workers is an important contribution not only to the organisation but also to the whole society. The 'social project' is closely connected to the

[4] As of 31 October 2019, OMRON has transferred all shares of OMRON Automotive Electronics Co., Ltd., which it holds, to Nidec Corporation.

Fig. 4.4 Overview of OAX

SDGs and shows its social significance to the employees. Furthermore, they strengthened the program by targeting both employees and their families, thus bringing joy to the workplace, as well as increasing employee satisfaction with life beyond the company. As a result, the turnover rate was lowered to 4.66%, well below the regional average of 9.65%.

OAX's turnover rate reduction project consists of a collection of many initiatives as described above, but the driving force behind is the corporate philosophy of 'respect for all'. The project leader, Adriana Guzman, said, 'I want you to understand work as a way to increase the value of your life, not as a duty'. This is an important example of the success of a Japanese corporate philosophy overseas. Guzman credits the significance of TOGA in creating a 'platform for global contribution'. OMRON employees worldwide are greatly inspired by knowing that various practices are conducted under the same corporate philosophy.

OAX's initiative has only just begun; they plan to develop it further. Since the organisational culture is changing through the cultivation of the corporate philosophy, they plan to change the employees' health management programme and apply human resource development initiatives to all fields in the future. Such in-house impetus can also be due to the effect of winning the TOGA Gold Award.

4.4 Characteristics of Emergent Responsible Management: Creating Social Value Beyond Economic Value

OMRON's corporate-philosophy-inspired projects are not narrowly defined CSR activities but rather, are initiatives based on the corporate philosophy of 'creating a better society' and the value of creating social needs by solving social issues. Thus, it can be understood as a means by which a company fulfils its responsibility for society. Since social value and economic value are different concepts, emphasising social value requires a different approach than general management. OMRON's corporate-philosophy-driven projects are good examples.

Economic value can be measured with indicators such as revenue or profit indicators. However, social values are subjective and can hardly be measured. Therefore, creating value by satisfying social needs cannot be planned in advance, and requires employees to think independently. In this way, OMRON's corporate-philosophy-driven projects, in which employees are directed to targets that cannot be determined in advance and that create social value for stakeholders, are typical examples of emergent responsible management.

In general, for corporate activities, there are such strong economic constraints that it is too difficult to legitimise the pursuit of solutions to social issues. However, these practices inspired by OMRON's principles can motivate employees to respond to social issues via TOGA. For example, regarding the OPC project, as Etani said, 'Developing it into a TOGA project has made it easier to pursue the social significance of the project'. Providing human resource to SMEs that are short in manpower and supporting the employment search of young people who are struggling to find jobs both address major social issues in Japan today. However, trying to figure this out in a traditional way would be probably stuck in the discussion of profitability. In such situations, the TOGA project has the power to steer employees towards the creation of social value.

From the impressions of the members who participated in the project, it can be seen that they have achieved a sense of accomplishment that cannot be obtained through general corporate operations. In particular, it is worth noting that by creating social value, the relationships between internal and external members have improved, and they become more aware of their own potential. This is obvious not only in the three projects introduced in this chapter, but also in many projects undertaken under the TOGA platform.

OMRON's corporate philosophy is abstract and does not suggest specific activities. However, the fact that as many as 31,000 projects have been implemented based on this abstract philosophy makes the emergent effect of these practices obvious. TOGA is growing into an activity that exceeds the original expectations. In this regard, Yamada stated the following:

> The "flag" we set up is to find a solution to social issues, so it's easy to get the support from other companies and our employees have come up with various ideas because they are useful to the world, which brings great benefit to our businesses as well. When it is designed

> to achieve sales, we will not get so many supporters, and I think that the idea of how to put the corporate philosophy into practice will be limited. I believe this is the benefit of our corporate philosophy. I am most grateful when it has the power to involve many people, so I never ask our employees to link it to business or to pursue profits in the short term. However, in the long term, it always affects on OMRON's performance, so I want to nurture it in the long run.[5]

Yamada's statement represents the full essence of TOGA. It is much easier to make full use of 'emergence' since TOGA aims to solve social issues. Besides, it does not have to be linked to short-term earnings, but it has a positive impact on OMRON's performance in the long run. One of the reasons why TOGA and other corporate-philosophy-driven projects are so successful is that Yamada and other top managements who fully shared the essence of the project give warm encouragement to employees who have worked hard. Thus, employees are able to exert more effort, and a virtuous cycle is created. Through dialogue between employees and top managements, the abstract corporate philosophy permeates practices and creates new connections outside the company. Through such activities, social value that exceeds economic value is created.

[5] This interview with Yamada was conducted by one of the authors (Kokubu) on February 27, 2019 as a project of Research Institute of Advanced Management. The interview was published in *Business Insight* No. 106 (July 2019).

Chapter 5
Bridgestone: Our Way to Serve

Hirotsugu Kitada and Katsuhiko Kokubu

Abstract To successfully promote emergent responsible management, it is important not only to design activities that employees spontaneously take part in, but also to link those to the management system of the entire company. This chapter sheds light on Bridgestone's Our Way to Serve approach, which is a good example to consider the relationship between individual initiatives and company-wide management mechanisms. Different from OMRON's initiatives to bring about new activities, Bridgestone tries to link the activities voluntarily undertaken at each site with the global management system. Our Way to Serve is a mechanism to translate the abstract corporate philosophy into concrete activities. It also serves as a guide for an individual employee's spontaneous activities. As a result, a flexible systematisation of management has been realised while giving full play to the spontaneity of each site. Bridgestone's efforts are excellent examples to demonstrate the implementation of emergent responsible management as a global company.

5.1 Bridgestone's Initiatives

Bridgestone was founded in 1931 by Shojiro Ishibashi. Bridgestone's tire business accounted for more than 80% of sales, and in the fiscal year ended December 2018, sales were approximately ¥ 3,650 billion. It is a highly internationalised company with an overseas sales ratio of over 80%, and the American market is the largest. One of the ultimate goals of management since 2013 has been to become 'a truly global company', and this was declared in the company's previous mid-term business plan. With approximately 180 productions and development bases in 26 countries worldwide, and operations in more than 150 countries, managing such an international organisation has become an important concern of this company.

Bridgestone established the concept of *Our Way to Serve* in 2017 to realise its corporate philosophy globally. This stems from the corporate mission, 'Serving Society with Superior Quality', which was enacted by the founder, Ishibashi. Through *Our Way to Serve*, Bridgestone suggests the direction for each member of the group to contribute to society.

K. Kokubu et al., *Emergent Responsible Management*, Kobe University Monograph Series in Social Science Research, https://doi.org/10.1007/978-981-19-0416-5_5

'Our', included in *Our Way to Serve*, expresses the desire of leaders and employees at all levels of various organisations to work together globally. At Bridgestone, employees have been voluntarily involved in social contribution activities at various business sites worldwide. *Our Way to Serve* aims to link these individual initiatives with the overall corporate strategy and to share these spontaneous initiatives throughout the organisation.

To successfully promote emergent responsible management, it is important not only to design activities that employees spontaneously take part in, but also to link those to the management system of the entire company. In that sense, Bridgestone's *Our Way to Serve* approach is a good example to consider the relationship between individual initiatives and company-wide management mechanisms.

The activities discussed in this chapter have been awarded within Bridgestone for their efforts to embody *Our Way to Serve*. However, prior to the enactment of *Our Way to Serve*, local employees had already been getting involved in various voluntary activities. As in the case of OMRON (Chap. 4), the award system is used in Bridgestone as a mechanism to promote emergent responsible management. However, while OMRON aims to create new activities, Bridgestone tries to link the activities voluntarily undertaken at each site with the global management system. As a result, a flexible systematisation of management has been realised while giving full play to the spontaneity of each site.

5.2 Corporate Philosophy and *Our Way to Serve*

5.2.1 Our Way to Serve

As mentioned earlier, Bridgestone has established *Our Way to Serve* based on its corporate mission, 'Serving Society with Superior Quality'. Bridgestone has defined *Our Way to Serve* as a CSR commitment, and set three priority areas, namely 'Mobility', 'People', and 'Environment', as specific issues to be addressed globally. Consequently, the abstract corporate philosophy has been transformed into a guiding principle for its activities in different times.

Christine Karbowiak, an executive director of Bridgestone, explained the effect of clearly defining the area of activity according to the external context as follows.

> There is a good deal of excitement and energy around *Our Way to Serve* as a simplified and enhanced CSR initiative. With *Our Way to Serve*, we are able to clearly define the areas where we as a company can contribute and really make a difference, which I see as one of this new initiative's primary benefits.[1]

In promoting emergent responsible management as well as sustainable management, it is important to clarify the values and visions of the company, and drawing reference

[1] *Bridgestone Sustainability Report* 2017–2018.

to the corporate philosophy can be an effective method. However, corporate philosophy is generally too abstract for developing activities. Therefore, it is necessary to devise a clear policy corresponding to the external environment.

Previously, at Bridgestone, the understanding of CSR and the approach towards initiatives varied among different regions. For example, in Japan, since the learning program provided by the headquarters was substantial, the understanding of CSR was advanced; however, it was recognised that the CSR voluntary initiatives were not that active. Conversely, in America and Europe, although they did not share a consistent understanding of CSR in Bridgestone due to fewer learning programs, voluntary initiatives for social contributions by employees were active. By establishing *Our Way to Serve* based on the corporate philosophy, Bridgestone attempted to relate such proactive voluntary initiatives to the overall corporate system.

Bridgestone is striving to incorporate the spontaneous and active efforts of its employees into the process of realising the corporate philosophy under the framework of *Our Way to Serve*. However, the emergent efforts of employees alone can barely make a difference to benefit the organisation. Therefore, an overall organisational design that can integrate such emergent efforts into routine management is necessary. Bridgestone's *Our Way to Serve* seeks to unify the directions of various activities, while leaving room for the diversity of individual engagement.

5.2.2 *Systems to Promote* Our Way to Serve

It has often been observed that a company's policy and its commitment to social contribution activities change dramatically when a manager is replaced. However, since Bridgestone's CSR activities are formally systematised and do not only overrely on who is in charge, it is easier for the company to continue consistent activities. Underpinning such activities, *Our Way to Serve* is positioned as the cornerstone of the management reform framework in the mid-term management plan, along with the Corporate Philosophy, Safety Declaration, Quality Declaration, and Environmental Declaration.

Bridgestone's approach to CSR is deeply embedded into the core of its management by systematising the promotion system of *Our Way to Serve* with the involvement of business management. Specifically, as shown in Fig. 5.1, the *Our Way to Serve* system consists of the Global CSR Promotion Committee and the Global Quality Management Committee, with representatives from each working group for the three priority areas (i.e. Mobility, People, and Environment), basic areas, and each Strategic Business Unit (SBU) and region.[2] *Our Way to Serve* initiatives are regularly reported to the top management through the Global CSR Promotion Committee.

---

[2] In addition to the three priority areas of 'Mobility', 'People', and 'Environment', Bridgestone sets the basic areas in *Our Way to Serve* scheme based on ISO2600, including compliance, fair competition, Business Continuity Planning (BCP), risk management, human rights and labour practices, occupational safety and health, procurement, and quality and customer value.

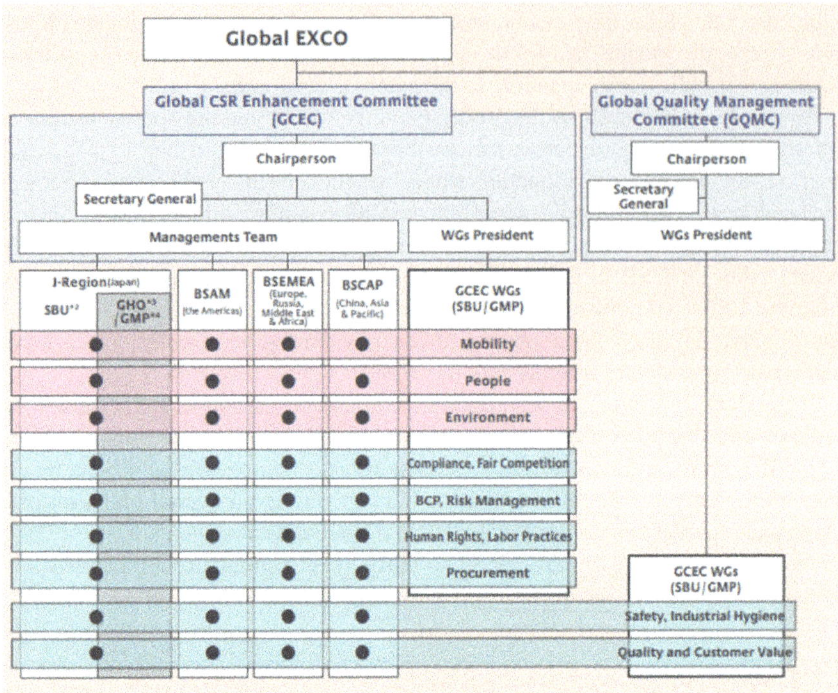

Fig. 5.1 Our Way to Serve system.[3] *Source* Website of Bridgestone

They report to the 'Global EXCO', an executive board with members including the CEO, three to four times a year. This report includes the basic approaches of the Group's overall CSR efforts, including prioritisation of issues to be addressed and strategies for sustainability. Figure 5.1 illustrates the system.

Bridgestone has adopted a step-by-step approach to introduce *Our Way to Serve* into the organisation. In 2017, the first year of the activity, efforts were made to raise awareness in the organisation, and in 2018, the focus was on deepening the understanding of the relationship between *Our Way to Serve* with individual day-to-day operations and the respective function required for the employees. Following such efforts, in 2019 and 2020, suitable plans were developed to promote the practice of specific activities. *Our Way to Serve* is a program that seeks to inspire the spontaneity and creativity of employees in the emergence of activities for social responsibility. Bridgestone recognised that it is time-intensive to diffuse and implement this concept throughout the organisation. Therefore, a road-map has been developed for organisational change.

[3] The abbreviations shown in Fig. 5.1 are as follows. Global EXCO: Global Executive Committee, SBU: Strategic Business Unit, GHO: Global Head Office, GMP: Global Management Platform, PA: Priority Areas, MF: Management Fundamentals (Basic area), BSAM: Bridgestone Americas, Inc., BE: Bridgestone Europe NV/SA, BSCAP: Bridgestone Asia Pacific, Ltd.

Regarding the promotion of *Our Way to Serve*, Bridgestone equally respects the autonomy of every region. In Japan, various efforts have been undertaken to broaden and deepen the understanding of *Our Way to Serve*, including e-learning programs and workshops conducted by selected key personnel from each workplace. Globally, representatives from each region (the Americas, Europe, Middle East, Africa, China, and the Asia Pacific) are selected to promote this initiative based on their regional characteristics.

5.2.3 Realising the Corporate Philosophy Through an Award System

Even before *Our Way to Serve* was established at Bridgestone, a few employees had voluntarily promoted social contribution activities. The most outstanding efforts have been awarded through the Bridgestone Group Awards. These awards were established in 2008 as a recognition programme open to all organisations and employees of the Bridgestone Group. It aims to raise employees' awareness of corporate activities based on the corporate philosophy and to foster a sense of unity among group employees as well as recognising accomplishments. In response to the establishment of *Our Way to Serve* in 2017, a specific award category for *Our Way to Serve* was included (Fig. 5.2).

Fig. 5.2 Bridgestone Group Awards Ceremony

The Bridgestone Group Awards are considered as an important management tool in Bridgestone, where the top management is responsible for appraisal and awarding. The selection process consists of two stages: a regional or divisional selection and a group-wide selection. In 2018, there were 294 entries, 30 of which qualified for the group-wide selection. Finally, seven activities were awarded, including cases related to the three priority areas of 'Mobility', 'People', and 'Environment'.

In the 'Mobility' category, a digital tool which was developed and deployed to contribute to Fleet customers for safer operations, higher economic benefits, and lower environmental impacts was selected. In the 'People' category, two cases were awarded; the project members from India established community trust through the construction of schools, provision of health check-ups, and road safety classes, resulting in building a sustainable relationship with the local community. The winner from Argentina worked together with its stakeholders including employees and business partners to deliver truckloads of donated supplies to rural schools lacking in resources. In the 'Environment' category, a case from Australia was selected, which entailed the development of conveyor belt splicing materials that do not use Volatile Organic Compounds.

The winners were selected not only for their contributions to society but also to the organisation such as the improvement of Bridgestone's brand awareness and its operations. Since the specific impact on society or the company is highly appreciated, the awarded activities tend to continue for a long time. There are no financial incentives for the winners, but they are awarded directly by the top management at the awards ceremony held in Japan and are honoured within the company.

Although the use of the award system is in common with OMRON, which aims to bring about emergent practices as discussed in Chap. 4, their approaches are obviously different. The Bridgestone Global Awards emphasise top management's recognition and approval of local activities throughout the whole group. The awarded activities are regarded as 'early adopters' that embody *Our Way to Serve.* By recognising outstanding activities through awards and sharing the best practice examples, the field of activities by the 'late majority' is expected to expand.

5.3 Bridgestone Group Awards Winners

5.3.1 Bridgestone India Community Support

Bridgestone India Community Support is an initiative of Bridgestone India, led by Ajay Sevekali and Kashiram Mestry, who received the Bridgestone Group Award in the 'People' category in 2018. This activity was awarded in the name of 'Developing Community Trust with Integrated Growth' for supporting the residents in Pune, India. Support for school construction, health checks, and road safety education was provided in Pune, where the tire plant is located. This project has been recognised for building a long-term trust relationship with the local community.

The initiative has started to resolve the trouble with local residents that arose due to the construction of the plant. The construction of an industrial park in Pune forced the residents to move out from their land, threatening their livelihoods. Several people blamed Bridgestone India, who was going to set up a factory in the industrial park and protests by the residents intensified with the support of village leaders, local politicians, and antisocial forces. Moreover, the local media also reported such reactions, increasing the contradictions due to a lack of mutual understanding.

To overcome this situation, Bridgestone India, with Sevekali and Mestry as key members, has been working to support the growth and development of the local people. During the implementation of various activities, they were keen to listen to the people's voices. By approaching the locals as one of their stakeholders, they came to understand the local issues such as regional security, education, employment, and health, and endeavoured to solve these problems with the involvement of the residents.

Bridgestone India did not hire the local residents directly but aimed to develop the community as a whole by stimulating the potential of the people. For example, the company helped high-potential individuals develop their entrepreneurial skills. Moreover, to develop a community with the involvement of residents, it is necessary to build a good relationship within the community. With this project, they strengthened cooperation with the local police and local municipality, and fought against certain antisocial forces and local leaders who were seeking to exploit the residents. As a result of these efforts, water supply was provided to about 1,400 households, schools were built, health was promoted, and traffic safety equipment was provided to the local police. In addition, over 100 new jobs, such as the transportation of tires or water and gardening, were created during the construction of the factory in Pune, which contributed to the stability of the local economy.

With their continued efforts in supporting the local community, local stakeholders became more amiable towards Bridgestone India. With their activities positively frequently reported in the media and awarded by local government, Bridgestone India got rid of the negative impressions that arose during the protests. As they continued their initiatives, even the ones who participated in the protests have become more supportive of Bridgestone India's activities (Fig. 5.3).

Regarding the Bridgestone Global Awards, Sevekali and Mestry, the leaders of the project, stated, 'We feel that the activities in support of the local residents have been recognised by the company, which encourages us to continue to work on realising the corporate philosophy of contributing to society.' Motivated by the awards, they are also considering expanding the scope of such activities in pursuit of building trust relationships with the local community.

Fig. 5.3 Donation from Bridgestone India to local elementary schools

5.3.2 Bridgestone Australia Leukaemia Foundation Support

Bridgestone Australia Leukaemia Foundation Support is an activity initiated by Bridgestone Australia and was awarded in the 'People' category in 2017. Bridgestone Australia has supported the Australia Leukaemia Foundation for 30 years since 1986. It began with the support for the Leukaemia Foundation by Peter Brock, the Australian racing legend, who was the Bridgestone brand ambassador at that time. Bridgestone Australia has expanded this activity throughout Australia, which was initially limited to the South Australian region.

This activity is now led by Joan Hayes. As the person in charge of this activity, Hayes engages personally in the activities of the Leukaemia Foundation, which supports a wide range of stakeholders in society. The continuance of the activity for 30 years can be considered as a result of the participation by numerous people who favour this activity. Local senior managers who occasionally take the lead also consider this activity beneficial for both society and Bridgestone. In this respect, the project applies both bottom–up and top–down approaches.

The Leukaemia Foundation is a non-profit organisation that supports leukaemia patients and their families, providing material and psychological support as well as funding for research to improve treatment. The activities are funded by non-governmental sources including public donations and financial support from companies such as Bridgestone. Bridgestone Australia is the only charity partner of the foundation, and its 30-year relationship is the longest in the field of corporate charity in Australia.

Fig. 5.4 Participation in the 'Light the Night' Event of the Leukaemia Foundation

Bridgestone Australia has implemented a variety of support activities, including providing vehicles to transport blood and patients, organising charity events for fundraising, and providing free accommodations for leukaemia patients and their families when receiving treatment. In recent years, in addition to these, the company has been supporting leukaemia research through the sale of specially designed blue valve caps for $3 per set, with all proceeds directly funding blood cancer research to enhance leukaemia treatment.

The Bridgestone Global Awards have also increased the awareness of the relationship between Bridgestone Australia and the Leukaemia Foundation. The award was also reported in the Leukaemia Foundation's annual report. This trust relationship, formed over the past 30 years, has been covered in local media and has greatly contributed to Bridgestone's regional reputation (Fig. 5.4).

5.4 Features of Emergent Responsible Management: Flexible Systematisation of CSR at the Global Level

In Bridgestone, emergent responsible management is featured by linking local independent actions with global management systems centred on *Our Way to Serve*—the commitment that reflects its corporate philosophy. In this way, Bridgestone has systematised its CSR flexibly as a global company. CSR activities are often dependent on a specific context, but the management generally requires a certain degree of standardisation. Though the global development of business, social responsibility differs in each business unit depending on the specific issues in the region and the cultural background of the people who work there. The key issue in management is the organisation of the various activities within the context of a diverse global society.

Based on its corporate philosophy, Bridgestone has established *Our Way to Serve* to have clarity on the policy of activities and further leaves room for diversity of individual engagement. By sharing samples of individual activity through the award system, these activities are flexibly incorporated into the group-wide CSR practices. As in the case of the Bridgestone Global Awards winners in India and Australia, organisations can enhance the quality of their activities by supporting their employees in practising the responsibilities they perceive. Furthermore, by evaluating and presenting them as excellent activities, they have made it possible for the employees to solve problems by deepening their own understanding of the challenges in CSR. If this were a project from headquarters, it may have been passively implemented and rigidly managed by the head office.

Recognising outstanding activities through the Bridgestone Global Awards not only increases the winners' motivation, but also promotes contribution to the society by the Group as a whole. The activities selected, reviewed and awarded by top management can be well recognised throughout the company. It is often difficult to internally evaluate activities that are not related to the core businesses. Gaining approval from top management is of great encouragement for the drivers of such initiatives. In addition, it motivates other employees who are also interested in activities involving social contribution.

Our Way to Serve is a mechanism to translate the abstract corporate philosophy into concrete activities. It also serves as a guide for an individual employee's spontaneous activities. Bridgestone has realised a flexible systematisation of CSR on a global scale through this concept. Bridgestone has improved the traditional CSR framework, in which the headquarters plays a central role in directing activities and promoting the achievement of the targets set in advance. The corporate philosophy that claims to contribute to society is not just a theme but serves as a management framework through which employees can practise their responsibilities. Bridgestone's efforts are excellent examples to demonstrate the implementation of emergent responsible management as a global company.

Chapter 6
Marui Group: Creating an Organisation Through Voluntary Participation

Hirotsugu Kitada and Katsuhiko Kokubu

Abstract The present chapter analyses the approach and the experience of Marui Group, which has been mainly engaged in apparel retail business and fintech service. This case study is an important and informative example that illustrates how to create a new management style by making the most out of spontaneity of employees. The emergent responsible management in Marui Group is conducted with official group project teams through an open application process. The approach of voluntary participation is deeply rooted in Marui Group's organisational culture, and Marui Group has been devoted to shaping such a perception to enhance employees' spontaneity. It is important to incorporate new perspectives into the organisation effectively by stimulating employees' motivation and spontaneity as well as reviewing issues from a sustainability perspective that are often overlooked in normal management. Marui Group's initiatives have fully taken these points into account.

6.1 Initiatives of Marui Group

Marui Group Co., Ltd., founded by Chuji Aoi in 1931, has been mainly engaged in apparel retail business and fintech service and made approximately 239 billion yen in sales in the fiscal year ending March 2018. Currently, the financial business based on fintech service has been strengthened; thus, it is shifting its focus to financial technology. Under the strong leadership of the current president, Hiroshi Aoi (the grandson of the founder), Marui Group is transforming its business model to combine retail and finance. In the meantime, the company has entered the content industry (e.g. animation and filmmaking), while strategically generating synergy with its core business, thus becoming a very innovative company in the industry.

Moreover, Marui Group has been devoted to developing 'co-creation sustainability management' to create value together with all stakeholders. Here, the 'stakeholders' do not only include customers, shareholders, investors, employees, and business partners but also involve the community and society. Thus, it aspires to create value in the retail business and financial technology business in cooperation with a wide

K. Kokubu et al., *Emergent Responsible Management*, Kobe University Monograph Series in Social Science Research, https://doi.org/10.1007/978-981-19-0416-5_6

range of stakeholders. Marui Group's sustainability initiatives are not only limited to social contribution but are also linked to its management and strategies.

To realise 'co-creation sustainability management' and create value together with stakeholders, Marui Group has adopted the concept of *inclusion.* Congruent with the direction set by the principles of the United Nations' Sustainable Development Goals (SDGs), *inclusion* is a very important concept when conducting 'co-creation sustainability management' to build an inclusive and flourishing society that offers happiness to all.

Marui Group defined four core themes to incorporate *inclusion* into management activities— customer diversity and inclusion, workplace inclusion, ecological inclusion, and co-creation corporate governance.[1] The 'official group project teams' discussed in this chapter address the first three theme. In the case of Marui Group's emergent responsible management, the target is well defined; thus, the problems are explicitly indicated by the company.

Sustainability initiatives resonate with the younger generation who value social responsibility. These initiatives are perceived to be effective in attracting the most talented graduates as well as those in the younger generation considering a career change. Moreover, sustainability initiatives have been highly praised by investors, with Marui Group being added to various indexes and receiving all kinds of awards. Therefore, the Group believes that its initiatives have contributed, to a certain degree, to the stability of the company's stock price.

As such, Marui Group places high priority on sustainability initiatives in corporate management, and Aoi has always played a leading role in this area as the president. For example, Aoi has participated in every editing meeting for the 'Co-creation Management Report', as well as the 'Co-Creation Sustainability Report', and appeared frequently in the report through interviews and dialogues with external experts. Besides, he also periodically explains the concept of *inclusion* at 'MARUI IR DAY,' an event for institutional investors. Hence, sustainability initiatives have been well integrated into management activities. In this chapter, as an example of the emergent responsible management in Marui Group, we will focus on the 'official group project teams' that employees can voluntarily participate in.

---

[1] Marui Group is committed to the SDGs with four core themes, namely, 'Customer Diversity and Inclusion' (Goals 1, 9, 10, and 11), 'Working Inclusion' (Goals 3, 4, 5, and 8), 'Ecological Inclusion' (Goals 7, 12, 13, and 15), and 'Co-creative Corporate Governance' (Goals 9, 16, and 17).

6.2 Enhance Employees' Spontaneity by Encouraging Voluntary Participation

Marui Group has formed group-wide committees and project teams with members who are interested in participating sustainability initiatives voluntarily.[2] The approach of voluntary participation is deeply rooted in Marui Group's organisational culture, and Marui Group has been devoted to shaping such a perception to enhance employees' spontaneity long before applying this method to sustainability activities.

Aoi has recognised voluntary participation as an important corporate culture since he was appointed as the president. It is when he saw some participants doze off in the medium-term management promotion meeting (where only executives attend and management policies are presented and shared) that he started to wonder how to make people not doze off in the meeting. The solution he came up with was voluntary participation. He thought that no one would fall asleep if the meetings were open to the company at large and those who wished to attend, instead of only executives or managers. Therefore, Marui Group started to receive applications and select participants throughout the company instead of limiting the meetings to managers or executives from 2015. Even newly recruited employees can participate if they want.

Consequently, the meeting was activated. It was such a good way that they also tried to introduce the approach of voluntary participation into the implementation of sustainability initiatives with various themes. Marui Group calls this kind of initiative as the 'official group project teams'. The Marui Mirai Project, which makes social contributions through its core business, has also been adopted as an official group project team. Aoi talks about the compatibility between the 'official group project teams' in which employees voluntarily participate and the social contribution activities as follows.

> Social contribution, such as environmental protection, is what everyone wants to make, so there is no need to enforce it. This also holds true for initiatives related to women's participation in workplace. No one, whether female or male, is adamantly opposed to the idea of creating an environment, culture, support system, and cooperative system that would allow more women to play an active role in management decision-making. We all want to cooperate in some way with no need to be forced. It is the same case regarding customers. There are few people who have no interest in setting up stores and providing products and services that can be enjoyed beyond disability, sexual orientation, and gender identity.[3]

Thus, the fact that top management recognises social contribution activities as something that employees want to do can be considered as one factor that makes this type of management work well. For instance, Aoi has expressed his opinion on why wellness management is necessary for the Marui Group, instead of simply leaving the matter to its employees. That is, this is what the employees want to do. Consequently,

---

[2] We describe details on the process regarding how Marui Group developed official group project teams with voluntary participation based on Aoi's lecture at the 5th Symposium on Healthcare and Management held at Hitotsubashi Hall on May 22, 2018.

[3] Same as Footnote 2.

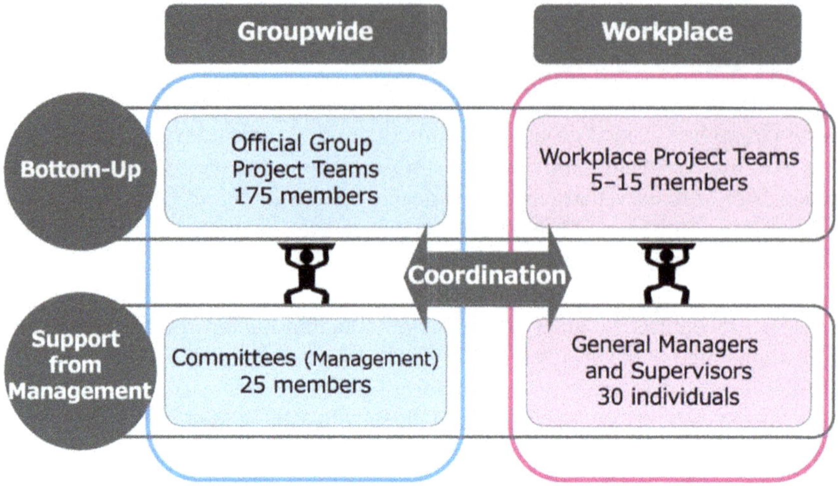

Fig. 6.1 Participants in the official group project teams. *Source* Website of Marui Group

this type of feedback from top management helps employees understand that what they want to do is desirable for the company, as well as for the stakeholders.

Official group project teams are open to voluntary participation by employees throughout the company, and the participants gather during working hours to work on a given theme. Project members are changed on an annual basis, and during the year they hold monthly meetings. As of September 2018, three project teams have been defined: (1) wellness and healthcare management, (2) Marui Mirai, and (3) diversity. The official group project team is made up of project members who voluntarily participate and committee members of senior managers who support their activities. There is also support from management, such as store managers or department heads, in every project member's workplace, and committee members are expected to act as coordinators between project members and their superiors. Aoi also recognises the importance of such corporate support as follows (Fig. 6.1).

> [Regarding corporate social activities,] the employees will voluntarily participate in projects as they want and the superior will create an environment that makes it easier for them to do it— for example, by allowing the participant to carry out the activities during working hours. For such group-wide initiatives, if participants hope to attend the activities for some time, senior managers should give priority to them regarding the arrangement of schedule and space. If such support could be provided, everyone would naturally focus on the project and make progress. Therefore, we conducted projects especially those related to the environment and social and governmental issues based on voluntary participation and employees' spontaneity.[4]

[4] Same as Footnote 2.

In this way, Marui Group introduces a system that emphasises spontaneity of employees through voluntary participation in 'Co-creation Sustainability Management.' There are three points that we need to pay attention to with regard to the mechanism for promoting spontaneity.

The first is the selection of participants in the project. The extent of people's interest in social issues varies; thus, maintaining high motivation for each activity is an issue to be solved, as the same with CSR management. Marui Group builds a system where people who are more motivated and interested can apply for the project through the selection process.

The second is to clarify the project period. In Marui Group, every month, one day is ensured and committed for the project, and project members are changed on an annual basis, thus helping the project progress more easily.

The third is the support team composed of senior managers. The problem of balancing daily work and sustainability activities is affected by the relationship between superiors and subordinates. To mitigate adverse effects, senior managers are involved as coordinators in the official group project team.

In this chapter, we look into the Wellness & Healthcare Management Project Team as an example to introduce how this official group project team works (various other projects have also been well implemented) (Fig. 6.2). For example, an initiative to make in-store signage more universal in design was implemented. This was also introduced at the co-creation sustainability explanatory forum as an example of the

Fig. 6.2 Meetings of the official group project team

Marui Mirai Project's activities. The Kinshicho store arranged an event to invite people with disabilities and their families to check the signage in the store, make improvement, and demonstrate the results.

In addition, as initiatives concerning lesbian, gay, bisexual and transgender (LGBT), there was also a try-on event for transgender individuals who were having problems in finding a suit for job-hunting purposes. Some employees who attended the LGBT events have improved their daily customer service. In the past, when women customers were choosing clothes or shoes in the men's area, they were used to say, 'Are you looking for a present?' However, now they will just ask 'May I help you?'.

Under the theme of *inclusion*, Marui engages in activities that involve stakeholders into the company's business while leveraging employees' spontaneity. The company aims at creating new value for the organisation by recognising social issues to be taken on by the whole company as major projects while encouraging employees' spontaneity in engaging in projects based on voluntary participation. In the next section, we will introduce the Wellness & Healthcare Management Project Team as a typical project.

6.3 Wellness Management Aimed at Improving Employees' Vitality

6.3.1 The Scheme of Wellness Management

Marui Group promotes wellness management as one of the four core themes of 'Working Inclusion' related to 'Co-creation Sustainability Management'. Wellness management, as part of labour management, is often implemented by the Human Resources Department, but it is also one of the important issues in CSR. For example, the GRI Standard[5] addresses the topic of health issues of labour in GRI103 (management approaches) and GRI403 (occupational health and safety). Wellness management can be regarded as an activity that covers both aspects of corporate management and sustainability initiatives.

As a policy of this activity, 'Marui Group is stepping up wellness initiatives aimed at energising employees that go beyond the basic approach of preventing illness (basic health). These initiatives focus on energising and empowering employees to increase productivity through changes in awareness and behaviour in order to drive improvements in corporate value and enable greater contributions to be made to society'.[6] Marui Group positions wellness management as a way to improve corporate value.

[5] The GRI standards provide guidance that organisations should follow when reporting their economic, environmental, and social effects to the public. Many companies worldwide, including Japan, have prepared sustainability reports in accordance with the GRI standards.

[6] From the website of Marui Group.

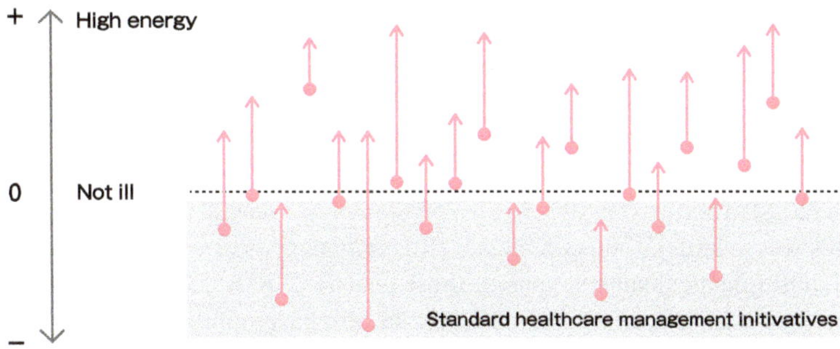

Fig. 6.3 Marui group's approach to wellness management. *Source* Website of Marui Group

Generally in Japan, wellness management for corporate employees aims to maintain and improve the health status of employees through medical examinations and awareness-raising activities, targeting at 'not ill' as shown in the middle of Fig. 6.3. However, as shown in this figure, this target level is set as zero; thus, Marui Group understands that such activities are passive. In addition to these, Marui Group focuses on active initiatives aimed at revitalising the organisation from the perspective of employees' health. For example, they intend to improve the quality of life of employees and revitalise the organisation by making employees aware of the importance of effective sleep and stress management methods.

In addition to the ideas of Aoi, these visions also reflect the opinions of Yuji Yamamoto, a physician who is also a member of the Marui Group's wellness management advisory board, as well as experts like Reiko Kojima, an industrial physician at the company and the executive officer and general manager of the Management Division. Yamamoto visualises the relationship between health and performance through data analysis. Kojima is also committed to creating the ideal conditions for sleep, diet, mood, and the like, to make employees work vigorously, in addition to the general work required as industrial physicians, such as medical examinations, consultations, and awareness-raising activities.

Hence, Marui Group involves internal and external experts into its management and incorporates ideas backed by their expertise into wellness management. In emergent responsible management, the process of 'exploring knowledge', where the employees play the leading role, is important. However, since it is different from general work, something that can motivate or guide the employees is needed. In the Marui Group's wellness and healthcare management project team, more specific directions have been suggested by incorporating the opinions of experts such as Yamamoto and Kojima. This is one of the important implications when regarding emergent responsible management as a process of exploring knowledge (discussed in Chap. 9).

In addition, the 'Resilience Program' is implemented by targeting senior managers in this company. Senior managers and store managers are supposed to participate in this project for one year to develop habits to energise their body, mood and mental state. The participation of top management in wellness initiatives has also led to an understanding and support of the official group project teams that employees are spontaneously working on.

In this way, Marui Group conducts wellness management within the organisation through multiple mechanisms. One of these is the wellness and healthcare management project, which is being promoted as an official group project team based on voluntary participation. So how do they actually encourage employees to assume a leading role, while taking the expertise of experts into account? We will discuss this point further in the next section.

6.3.2 The Activity of the Wellness and Healthcare Management Project Team

The concept of voluntary participation is remarkably compatible with the wellness and healthcare management project, and there were more than five times as many applicants have applied. The members selected through the submitted reports gather throughout Japan once a month and participate in a meeting for learning and dialogue on healthcare promotion over a day. Even though they participate voluntarily, the time they spend on the activities is treated as working hours. Participants try to find out what Marui Group should do in terms of wellness management while providing feedback on what they have learned there to their workplaces and personal lives.

Projects are usually implemented based on an annual schedule. The activities in the first phase of the Wellness & Healthcare Management Project were carried out from October 2016 to September 2017, in which they discussed the Marui Group's vision for wellness management. In the second phase, from October 2017 to September 2018, based on the vision established in the first phase, the team explored how to build a system to diffuse wellness management throughout the organisation.

In the second phase of the project, the design of specific methods including KPIs was initially discussed. However, Aoi indicated in the interim presentation conducted in March (six months after the start of the project) that the link between the wellness initiatives and the results, as well as performance, was not clear. He suggested that it might be important for the members to take action to demonstrate the link to the results. After fully discussing these points, they decided that each member would explore the actual situation through their own proactive actions as the first priority for demonstrating the effectiveness of the wellness activities.

After that, each member took action on healthcare promotion in their workplace and examined the effect and its impact on management. For example, Kohei Takahashi of Hakata Marui, one of the participants in the second phase of the project, tried to keep a record of daily sleep hours, when breakfast is taken, and the performance of daily business activities, and analysed the relevance. This is inspired by a lecture given by industrial physician Kojima regarding ideal sleep hours.

Takahashi learned the effects of adequate sleep, healthy eating, and exercising on efficiency at work, and said that having breakfast and exercising in the morning would help employees become more effective in serving customers. In addition, he also recognised from his own experience that adequate sleep would help prevent a decrease in concentration. He encouraged other members of the workplace to check their health condition every morning to lift their mood, leading to the promotion of wellness management in the workplace (Fig. 6.4).

Takahashi realised that what he learned from the lecture of the Wellness & Healthcare Management Project—which is to change his sleeping habits and diet—could help improve his daily work. However, it was difficult to persuade people around to feel the same way. Therefore, he started with what he could and attempted to enlist those around him as he sought solutions. For example, for the collection of data on health and work, he started with just a few people on a trial basis, and then the activity spread to all employees on the same floor after they saw that those participating in the trial were working vigorously and achieving results.

In addition to recording and examining the relationship between health and performance, Takahashi also developed a tool named story map at the workplace. This tool aims to contribute to understanding the importance of healthcare by drawing a diagram to show the relationship between the effects of certain actions. Taking

Fig. 6.4 Morning exercises by Takahashi and His Colleagues at Hakata Marui

smoking cessation as an example, we can be conscious of its influences by thinking about the connections. As negative effects, we may feel 'irritated' and 'get angry and fat' more easily, which eventually leads to 'sickness'. Regarding positive effects, we can start from 'thinking about health' and 'medical expenses', which means that by giving up smoking we can 'reduce costs' and 'improve working performance', thus we can 'have time' for 'self-development'. By addressing and working on this problem, participants are expected to gain a deeper understanding of how it affects themselves and others, as well as the mechanism behind it. Using a story can make it easier to understand a comprehensive model of the causal relationship between the effects of sleep and diet on work performance (as mentioned above). In this way, Takahashi spread throughout the organisation what he learned from his own experience and what he thought is useful.

Takahashi said that he had become more sensitive to external information on healthcare promotion by participating in the official group project team. Sensitivity (or exposure) to new information is also effective for emergent activities that are based on connections with internal and external stakeholders, and it is expected that such connections will improve the organisation's ability to explore knowledge.[7]

Exposure to new information encourages employees who work at the front line to engage more in activities that promote wellness management, which further encourages other employees to get involved. Takahashi stated that involving the people around you is not easy when proceeding with the activities, but if an activity was requested by the head office with a top-down approach, it would probably be even more difficult to achieve cooperation. In fact, Kojima, an industrial physician, claimed that in many other companies, healthcare promotion courses may have little effect on the organisation because only a small number of interested people participate repeatedly, which is too weak for internal penetration. However, Marui Group constructs a unique management system to promote employees' spontaneity with official group project teams based on voluntary participation, as in this wellness initiative.

6.4 Characteristic of Emergent Responsible Management: Management Inspiring Employees' Spontaneity

The emergent responsible management in Marui Group is conducted with official group project teams through an open application process, forming a unique management style that promotes the spontaneity of employees. Aoi regards sustainability initiatives as 'what everyone wants to do,' and then manages to create an environment where employees can make the most out of their spontaneity.

Such top management's understanding has something in common with infinite responsibility. The project envisioned by Marui Group is 'what the employees want to

[7] See Chap. 9 for a more detailed explanation.

do' for society, so the motivation should have emanated from a sense of responsibility inherent in human nature, regardless of whether they have noticed it or not. The initiative of Marui Group has successfully captured employees' feelings.

The members of the official group project team are provided with some place and some time when they can regularly put aside daily work and concentrate on the target activity. In addition, by setting up support members consisting of senior managers, an environment that facilitates cooperation within the organisation is also put into place. The design of an environment that encourages the spontaneity of project participants and the process of 'emergence' is a good point of reference for a model of emergent responsible management.

Marui Group provides expertise to employees to help them specify their ideas through regular meetings. This practice does not only improve the level of activity but also clarifies the relationship between the organisation and the social issues it addresses. As a result, in the case of the Wellness & Healthcare Management Project, the participants become the leaders of healthcare promotion at each workplace and help improve the quality of life of other employees while involving the people around them.

Through practice, the interaction between experts and members has been created, and a new management style has been formed as a result. The process is designed so that participants can repeatedly engage in trial and error by clarifying the cycle of gaining knowledge and its demonstration in practice, which can also be considered as an effort made to encourage employees' spontaneity.

It is also important to note that the motivation for the activities was elevated to a higher level so that the members' 'desire to do' naturally led to 'something that is good for the company'. To elicit such motivation, it is also important that Aoi has a clear vision of inclusive management and continues to convey the message that he links sustainability with management at the strategic level. Thus, top management has promoted emergent bottom-up activities.

In this way, Marui Group has created a new management style by making the most out of the spontaneity of employees in the official group project team. It is an important point for emergent responsible management to incorporate new perspectives into the organisation effectively by stimulating employees' motivation and spontaneity as well as reviewing issues from a sustainability perspective that are often overlooked in normal management. Marui Group's initiatives have fully taken these points into account.

Chapter 7
Yahoo Japan: Problem-Solving Engine

Mitsunobu Ando and Hirotsugu Kitada

Abstract This chapter focuses on the Tohoku Restoration Support Project by Yahoo Japan, one of the top-ranking companies that provide comprehensive IT Service in Japan. To do this, after having introduced the company's background information, the evolution from supporting disaster restoration to solving-social-problem business is briefly introduced with two examples: the initiatives of Ishinomaki Base and the activities of Fisherman Japan. These activities embody the company's corporate philosophy of a 'Problem-solving Engine'. Based on this philosophy, employees on site are supposed to set goals and perform self-evaluation, and the company has granted great discretion and freedom to employees to conduct these activities. Therefore, highly flexible organisational management is a feature of Yahoo Japan's emergent responsible management. In this way, not only the independence and spontaneity of employees are respected, the system to develop such ability is harnessed as well. Yahoo Japan's case shows that emergent responsible management can also be successful as a business model.

7.1 Yahoo Japan's Initiatives

Yahoo Japan Corporation (hereinafter, Yahoo Japan),[1] an information technology (IT) service company founded in 1996, focuses on portal site management, Internet advertising, and e-commerce services. Yahoo Corporation was established in the United States in March 1995, and Yahoo Japan Corporation was established in January 1996 in collaboration with Soft Bank to expand internet services in Japan. In the fiscal year 2017, the business scale was 897.1 billion yen in sales and 185.8 billion yen in operating profit, making it one of the top-ranking, comprehensive IT service companies in Japan.

Yahoo Japan has set its mission as a 'Problem-solving Engine' and aims to solve social problems by using IT. The company declared in its integrated report: 'Yahoo! JAPAN continues to pursue initiatives to solve problems in people's daily lives and

[1] On 1 October 2019, Yahoo Japan Corporation transitioned to a holding company structure and changed its name to Z Holdings Corporation.

K. Kokubu et al., *Emergent Responsible Management*, Kobe University Monograph Series in Social Science Research, https://doi.org/10.1007/978-981-19-0416-5_7

problems facing society by leveraging information technologies. As a 'Problem-solving Engine',[2] Yahoo! Japan will contribute to people and society through its various businesses'. As with CSR activities, the company has also launched various projects under the same mission.

Yahoo Japan sets 'Creating the Future with Four UPDATEs' as its concept of CSR and specifies the material issues, namely, 'Developing an IT Society', 'Supporting Disaster Relief and Social Issues', 'Building a Society Where everyone Can Play an Active Role', and 'Working toward a Sustainable Society'. Up to now, more than 45 CSR projects have been launched in these four areas. All projects have contributed to solving social issues using Yahoo Japan's platforms and services. The Corporate Social Responsibility Business Division of Social Responsibility Promotion Group, led by the officer in charge of CSR, plays a central role in promoting CSR.

Among these, we will introduce the Tohoku Restoration Support Project in this chapter. This project is conducted mainly by the members of the Tohoku team in the CSR Promotion Office of the corporate headquarters. As an IT company in Tokyo, the reason for Yahoo Japan's involvement in regional restoration activities (Tohoku region) lies in its previous efforts in restoration support for disaster-stricken regions. Specifically, Yahoo Japan launched the 'Yahoo Disaster Information' service in 2005 and established 'The Yahoo Fund' for supporting disaster victims in 2006. Therefore, Yahoo Japan was able to launch 'East Japan Earthquake Emergency Disaster Fundraiser' exactly on the day of the earthquake on March 11, 2011, by taking the advantage of its previous initiatives.

7.2 From Supporting Disaster Restoration to Solving-Social-Problem Businesses

Yahoo Japan's support for restoration following the Great East Japan Earthquake was initially undertaken by the branch 'Yahoo Ishinomaki Base' (hereinafter, Ishinomaki Base) in Ishinomaki city in Miyagi prefecture. Projects such as 'Fisherman Japan', 'Tour de Tohoku', and 'Yale market' (the former restoration department) that were launched by Ishinomaki Base are still on-going. Most of the restoration support activities are aimed at social contribution, little of which directly leads to economic value. However, some of the projects were taken over and continually managed by the special department of Tokyo Head Office, with an increasing profit.

In Yahoo Japan, CSR activities are managed on a project basis, but unlike in a normal business, there is no obligation to maximise profits. If the minimum amount of profit is secured, priority can be given to solving social issues and creating social value. Such a sense of purpose and process is remarkably close to the social business, which makes it a successful business model. A few years after the disaster, many companies have withdrawn from disaster restoration activities. However, Yahoo

[2] From the Yahoo's website and its integrated report (2018 edition).

Japan's projects are still active because they are also earning profits and do not just remain charitable.

Takuya Hasegawa and Koichi Sunaga from the CSR Promotion Offices in Ishinomaki Base started this project immediately after the earthquake. Hasegawa is a key person in Yahoo Japan, who in addition to managing this project, is also involved in various activities such as media coverage, lectures in universities, and book publication.[3] In April 2012, Hasegawa and Sunaga established the 'Yahoo Restoration Support Office' (renamed Ishinomaki Base later). At the outset, there were no specific instructions from senior management regarding the activities, and they started by visiting the site in person and planning the activities by themselves. The president at that time, Manabu Miyasaka, advised them to 'Try what Yahoo can do', which still guides their actions today.

Initially, they sought to help people who were directly affected by the earthquake through the power of IT and business. However, they gradually shifted the priority to local issues following the disaster, rather than limit themselves to recovery efforts from the damage directly caused by the earthquake. For example, Fisherman Japan has been launched as a project from Ishinomaki to promote fisheries in Japan, rather than helping fishermen only in Ishinomaki. To make fisheries a sustainable industry, Fisherman Japan has been engaged in activities such as training fishermen and expanding sales channels, which are beyond the scope of restoration activities.

In traditional CSR, companies tend to prioritise engagement with direct stakeholders (shareholders, investors, employees, business partners, customers, etc.). However, with the activities in Ishinomaki, under the 'Problem-solving Engine' mission, Yahoo was able to identify and involve previously unrelated stakeholders in the region to solve social issues and create social value. They were also able to gather support from a variety of organisations, including their competitors, for their highly social projects. For example, in addition to their own funding, financial support was gained from other companies' start-up support programs as well as government agencies and municipalities, and crowdfunding was also used for the launch of Fisherman Japan. Yahoo engages with a wide range of social groups and stakeholders to obtain funding and develop social activities. The purpose of resolving social issues beyond one organisation makes it possible to procure resources from other companies for its own CSR projects.

The following section introduces two projects as examples of emergent responsible management in Yahoo Japan: the initiatives of Ishinomaki Base and the activities of Fisherman Japan, in which its staffs are heavily involved. These activities are not CSR activities undertaken by the entire company of Yahoo Japan but rather, a problem-solving business led by a small number of elite employees locally.

---

[3] Hasegawa, T. (2014) *Ten Times the Challenge, Five Times the Failure and Twice the Success, A Little Bit of Sticking Out, More Connecting: How Yahoo works*, Toyo Keizai Inc (in Japanese).

7.3 Problem-Solving Engine in Practice

7.3.1 Yahoo Ishinomaki Base

Ishinomaki Base is a strategic regional branch that Yahoo Japan set up in July 2012. It was established to bring about projects to interact with the local community, in anticipation of medium- to long-term activities, rather than being a temporary base for restoration support. At the time of our survey, Ishinomaki Base had three full-time employees. They were previously situated at the Tokyo Head Office, but have now moved to Ishinomaki for the project. A variety of projects were launched from this base, starting with the support for restoration following the Great East Japan Earthquake. Basic CSR activities, including corporate governance and supply chain management, are conducted by other CSR-related teams and departments, based in the Tokyo Head Office. Ishinomaki Base, in principle, is independent from those activities and focuses on activities in Ishinomaki (Fig. 7.1).

Ishinomaki Base is Yahoo Japan's Tohoku office and is, as well as, a co-working space available for anyone to use. Normally, the security of an IT company is extremely strict, as it is at Tokyo Head Office of Yahoo Japan. However, the Ishinomaki Base is a workspace where local people have unrestricted access. To promote open innovation, Yahoo Japan built a collaboration space called 'LODGE' in its Tokyo Head Office building in 2016 based on the Ishinomaki Base experience. Ishinomaki Base uses furniture made by the local manufacturers, which is also used in

Fig. 7.1 Founding members of Ishinomaki Base

the Tokyo Head Office. The concept and atmosphere of open space which worked well in Ishinomaki has also been adopted by Tokyo. Taking advantage of the small number of people, Ishinomaki Base also serves as a place for pilot projects, new office features and systems like LODGE, as it is far from the headquarter with a greater degree of freedom.

The establishment of Ishinomaki Base was decided by top management, but the decision-making about activities in practice is left to the employees. Instead of a top–down business plan developed in advance, the activities are adjusted and operated while addressing stakeholders and social issues at the workplace, and the goals are flexibly adjusted. This achieves a good balance between the top–down and bottom–up approaches. Yahoo Japan's open culture provides the foundation for accepting a flexible organisation such as Ishinomaki Base.

The flexibility to engage in activities at Ishinomaki Base is also reflected in the change of purposes of the activities. After starting restoration support activities, which were mainly philanthropic initially, Ishinomaki Base gradually shifted its focus to local issues by making minute changes in its activities constantly. Organisational management requires flexibility to respond to social momentum and changes; when the prerequisites for organisational activities change, it must respond to those changes. Managing the project in a way that emphasises the independence of employees and enables real-time decision-making at the workplace is useful for solving social issues, as opposed to a top–down style of management where the decision-makers (top management) are not always present. Hasegawa, an early member of the Ishinomaki Base said, 'My birthday is March 11, same as the day when the earthquake happened, and I am destined to support the victims of the Great East Japan Earthquake.' His tenacity on restoration support was strong. However, the focus of activities at the Ishinomaki Base were shifted to regional issues without sticking to just disaster recovery. In July 2018, when we visited the base, the word 'earthquake recovery' was seldom used in daily business or everyday life, and social interest was shifted to regional revitalisation and social business support.

By developing their activities through Ishinomaki Base, they were able to perceive the problem more along the lines of reality than those in the CSR offices of other companies that were conducting social support activities at their headquarters in a large city. For example, activities rooted in the local community, such as sponsoring a local festival, were also an opportunity to deepen relationships with the community. Although philanthropic activities, such as sponsorship, tend not to be given much importance due to its difficulty in generating economic benefits, Hasegawa believed that there were still some activities that needed to be constant. The members of Ishinomaki Base complement Yahoo's CSR activities by contributing to the community through individual activities that can only be seen through direct interaction with stakeholders. Indeed, the network formed by the steady contribution to the community was the foundation of the emergent activities.

7.3.2 Fisherman Japan

Fisherman Japan was established in May 2014 to revitalise the fisheries industry in the Sanriku area in Miyagi. With a mission to 'become the first runner who implements 'The New 3K[4] (Kakkoii⟨attractive⟩, Kasegeru⟨profitable⟩, Kakushinteki⟨innovative⟩)' in the fishing industry from the sea of Sanriku', young fishermen in Sanriku are encouraged to participate in the activity. The project involves various stakeholders beyond the boundaries of regions and industries and has expanded the sales channels to overseas, proposing an approach to fisheries that will advance to the next generation (Fig. 7.2).

In recent years, Fisherman Japan's efforts have been covered by various business media, popularising it more than before. Among Ishinomaki Base's projects, Fisherman Japan has attracted the greatest attention. Hasegawa and his colleagues have been involved since the project was launched. This project would not have started without Yahoo Japan's support. Annual sales have reached hundreds of millions of yen, and it has generated economic impacts in the region through job creation and increase in distribution volume. The company has also obtained certification, such as the Marine Stewardship Council (MSC) certification,[5] and aims at a multifaceted

Fig. 7.2 Founding member of Fisherman Japan

[4] Usually, 3K means harsh (Kitui), dirty (Kitanai) and dangerous (Kiken).

[5] The marine stewardship council (MSC) has provided a blue fish mark certification label as 'sea eco-level' for seafood harvested after protecting marine fishery resources.

development of fisheries, with the improvement of brand awareness and product development.

Fisherman Japan is an independent organisation, a business alliance of Yahoo Japan with no capital relationship. With two part-time and ten full-time staff members for its operation, Ishinomaki Base is totally independent from Yahoo Japan with a diverse membership including fishermen and fresh fish retailers between whom a conflict of interest usually exists. MBA holders (unusual in Japanese fisheries) are also involved in the management team. They conduct commercial activities, including fish distribution and restaurant management, as well as non-profit activities, such as increasing the number of fishermen. Private fishing associations of this size that have business alliances with various companies and organisations (besides Yahoo Japan) are rare in Japan.

The main activities are training fishermen and expanding sales channels of marine products. The local seafood market is shrinking, so increasing the number of fishermen would lead to excessive competition. However, if they succeed in expanding sales channels, a shortage of producers (fishermen) might occur, resulting in unexpected drops in product supplies in the future. There are some NPOs that support fisheries or marine product suppliers, but in many cases they address either issue, not both. Since their support activities are not organised in a comprehensive way, this kind of project does not work well enough in many rural places. Fisherman Japan has noticed this issue and tries to promote both activities in a balanced way.

Hasegawa was worried that if they promoted their activities in the name of 'restoration', it would eventually end. Therefore, he cogitated about the essence of the issues in the Ishinomaki area and narrowed it down to the issue of 'fishing'. Sanriku is one of the world's three largest fishing grounds, along with Norway and Newfoundland. It is home to a large variety of high-quality fishes where fishing used to be one of the key industries.

Certainly, the tsunami washed away the city, which exacerbated the challenges faced by the Sanriku community. However, before the tsunami in the Sanriku region, the local community had already been swamped with a stagnant economy due to the aging population. Ishinomaki Base has been searching for targets through an emergent process of exploration and by understanding social issues through dialogue with local people. Hasegawa said that if they could build a business that contributed to solving local issues beyond restoration support, it was reasonable for private companies in Tokyo such as Yahoo Japan to be involved in this project. The driving force was not the willingness of top management, but the desire of employees to solve the problems found in the local community. Undeniably, it is one of the emergent projects under the initiative of employees on site.

7.4 Characteristic of Emergent Responsible Management: Management Respecting the Independence of Employees

Yahoo Japan has granted great discretion and freedom to employees in their CSR activities. As a result, the organisation has been managed by giving priority to the creation of business opportunities. This is compatible with *self-management*, *wholeness*, and *evolutionary purpose*, which are described as the core concepts of a *Teal Organisation.*[6] The employees' CSR activities in this company embody the corporate philosophy of a 'Problem-solving Engine'. Based on this philosophy, employees on site are supposed to set goals and perform self-evaluation. Although a major business change in day-to-day operations requires the approval of a superior in their department, there are almost no specific instructions concerning operations, and employees are independently engaged in on-site activities on a daily basis. Instead of focusing on KPIs, only broad goals are set, and detailed targets and roles are flexibly modified according to the progress. Highly flexible organisational management is a feature of Yahoo Japan's emergent responsible management.

In Yahoo Japan's activities, the independence and spontaneity of employees are not only respected, the system to develop such ability is harnessed as well. Emergent responsible management does not function smoothly just by delegating authority and increasing discretion; only with the active and spontaneous activities of each employee can discretion be effective. At Ishinomaki Base, employees manage all the activities (except part of the reporting work) by themselves along with their daily responsibility. Yahoo Japan has established a business process that allows employees to first try and adjust or even give up if some problem occurs subsequently. Such a corporate culture also contributes to the development of employees' spontaneity. Since there are no direct instructions from superiors, employees on site have the right to determine what to do and how to do it by themselves, which may reduce work stress. However, it is always necessary for the employees to take a proactive approach. Although it may be difficult for a large, organised company to adopt such a system, this field-driven process is exactly a typical management style for emergent responsible management.

Yahoo Japan's corporate philosophy of a 'Problem-solving Engine' calls for employees to contribute to solving social issues beyond CSR. The activities of Ishinomaki Base have been developed to contribute to the achievement of the company's mission, reflecting its corporate philosophy. However, due to great individual discretion and freedom, individual differences in activities determined by themselves may exist and hinder overall optimisation.

To overcome this problem, a promising approach is to strike a balance between discretion and overall optimisation by propagating the corporate philosophy. As a result of great discretion, operations are often run on a project basis with a small

[6] Laloux presents three breakthroughs from traditional management as follows: self-management, wholeness, and evolutionary purpose. Laloux, F. (2014) *Reinventing Organization: A Guide to Creating Organization Inspired by the New Stage of Human Consciousness*, Nelson Parker.

number of people, and the work becomes largely dependent on personal knowledge or experience. At Yahoo Japan, after the project has been put on the right track, the management will be handed over to Tokyo Head Office, leaving the operation to employees on site, which allows the activities to continue with flexibility. The fact that the corporate philosophy has been endorsed by all members of the company has smoothed the process of handing over the business model that was established based on local issues to the Tokyo Head Office. Although starting from restoration support activities, it was understood that such short-term charity activities could not be sustained without focusing on addressing essential social issues in Tohoku and converting them into opportunities for business, which was also a factor in promoting internal collaboration. From the beginning, social issues were properly identified at the Ishinomaki Base centred on the corporate philosophy.

In this way, Yahoo Japan's emergent responsible management is positioned as a part of CSR, but its content goes far beyond the scope of CSR and is an entirely new way of management. Ishinomaki Base, with the support of the head office, developed a management style in which employees can work independently. Approaching social issues while creating new connections by allowing employees to think and act on their own can be regarded as a typical model of emergent responsible management.

Furthermore, Yahoo Japan's initiatives created employment as an economic benefit for the Tohoku region. In traditional CSR, donations were a major approach for contributing to local communities. However, donations are temporary. In contrast, by creating new jobs and activities, the impact will continue. Furthermore, the continuous activities of Ishinomaki Base have also contributed to improving Yahoo Japan's reputation. Brand awareness is also promoted, with increasing number of people becoming aware of the project from the book written by the members of the Ishinomaki Base and the coverage by the media. Yahoo Japan is effectively appealing to the society with the uniqueness of the project and its impact on society.

Moreover, the ancillary economic benefits associated with the project are not insignificant. For example, since the number of participants of the bicycle event 'Tour de Tohoku' (an activity initiated by Ishinomaki Base) has been increasing every year, road bikes have been selling well in the Tohoku area, and the number of bicycle shops has increased. The positive impact of the activities in Ishinomaki over the past six years is immense. Undoubtedly, these are opportunities and achievements created by employees who are not bound by the traditional framework of CSR centred on risk management with a top–down management style and who are aware of the social issues and forge ahead to solve them deliberately. Yahoo Japan's case shows that emergent responsible management can also be successful as a business model.

Chapter 8
Mitsubishi Heavy Industries Group: The 'Kizuna' Activities

Kimitaka Nishitani and Katsuhiko Kokubu

Abstract The aim of this chapter is to provide a discussion of the business case of Mitsubishi Heavy Industries Group, which is the largest machine manufacture in Japan and known as the core company of Mitsubishi Group along with MUFG bank and Mitsubishi Corporation. This case study illustrates the application of emergent responsible management by investigating the Kizuna Activities, which not only contribute to society but also aim at increasing employee satisfaction. Although the Kizuna Activities are originally started to increase employee satisfaction, it is important to note that while actually fulfilling social responsibilities, employee satisfaction has also been improved, leading to human resource development and a sense of organisational unity. To conduct such activities, it is important to have a system in which activities can be continued to solve social issues as long as employees have a strong will. The increase in employee satisfaction resulting from the Kizuna Activities guarantees this, and at the same time it indicates that emergent responsible management can also have a positive effect on the main business.

8.1 Activities of Mitsubishi Heavy Industries Group

The Kizuna Activities (Kizuna means bond/ties in Japanese) originated from activities that were carried out at the former Engine Business Unit, a thermal power generation related product division, of Mitsubishi Heavy Industries, Ltd. (hereafter, Mitsubishi Heavy Industries). The merger of the thermal power generation related product divisions of both Mitsubishi Heavy Industries and Hitachi, Ltd. in 2014 leads to the establishment of Mitsubishi Hitachi Power Systems, Ltd. as an affiliate of Mitsubishi Heavy Industries. Since then, activities have continued by Mitsubishi Hitachi Power Systems and the power domain of Mitsubishi Heavy Industries that cover the entire power generation system (including nuclear power and renewable energy). For this reason, this chapter describes the operating body of the activity as 'Mitsubishi Heavy Industries Group'.

Mitsubishi Heavy Industries is headquartered in Tokyo and Yokohama, and is the largest machine manufacturer in Japan with main businesses in power systems; industry and infrastructure; aircraft, defence, and space. It is also known as the core

K. Kokubu et al., *Emergent Responsible Management*, Kobe University Monograph Series in Social Science Research, https://doi.org/10.1007/978-981-19-0416-5_8

company of Mitsubishi Group along with MUFG Bank and Mitsubishi Corporation. As of March 2018, the company had 80,652 employees, with sales of 4,110.8 billion yen, and net income of 70.4 billion yen on a consolidated basis.

Mitsubishi Heavy Industries originated in 1884 when its predecessor, Mitsubishi Mail Steamship Company, leased the government-owned Nagasaki Shipyard and started the shipbuilding business under the name Nagasaki Shipyard & Machinery Works thereafter. In 1934, the company was renamed as Mitsubishi Heavy Industries with the business expanding into manufacturing ships, heavy machinery, airplanes, and rolling stocks. In 1950, after World War II, Mitsubishi Heavy Industries was temporarily divided into three entities—West Japan Heavy Industries, Central Japan Heavy Industries, and East Japan Heavy Industries—by the dissolution of the Zaibatsu. However, they were reconsolidated in 1964 and reborn as (the new) Mitsubishi Heavy Industries.

Mitsubishi Hitachi Power Systems is a machine manufacturer that mainly provides thermal power generation related products, with the head office in Yokohama. As of March 2018, the company had 19,574 employees on a consolidated basis.

Mitsubishi Heavy Industries Group has stated in its corporate philosophy that '[...] contribute to societal progress through our business', and its corporate activities reflect the philosophy of social responsibility. Therefore, while many activities are carried out in the scope of CSR, some other activities also reflect social responsibility even if they are not classified as CSR activities. The Kizuna Activities, which not only contribute to society but also aim at increasing employee satisfaction, are the latter activities. The Kizuna Activities relies completely on the independence of employees from the selection of social issues to their solutions without limiting the responsibilities of the company. Therefore, they can be considered as an activity of emergent responsible management. In this chapter, we will investigate this Kizuna Activities from the perspective of emergent responsible management.

8.2 Kizuna: From Today, Always Friends

In 2006, the former Engine Business Unit of Mitsubishi Heavy Industries started activities aimed at improving customer satisfaction and increasing employee motivation. Through these activities, several problems were recognised, including the subdivision of the organisation due to the specialisation and sophistication of work, the weakening of human relations and cooperative relations in the company resulting from the tendency to avoid mutual interference between employees, and the trend that certain individuals are prioritised over others because of meritocracy and the performance-based system. The unit was concerned that such problems may cause a lack of employees' motivation to work, consideration for customers and colleagues, and a spirit of affiliation, which may affect the quality of work. As a key to solving such problems, attention has been focused on improving the mental health of employees, that is, increasing employee satisfaction.

For example, if employees can set their own desired themes and demonstrate their own abilities to achieve the goals while autonomously tackling the problem, employee satisfaction can be increased. In addition, it is expected that the effect will be further enhanced by contributing to others and working together with supporting members who have similar aspirations. Following this logic, they plan to improve the quality of work through increased employee satisfaction resulting from making social contributions. Furthermore, an increasing number of people have begun to appreciate this plan as an opportunity for human resource development.

It is ideal to increase employee satisfaction through the main business, but this may be difficult for various reasons. The employees' duties in their main business may not always exactly match their aspirations. Besides, there is no guarantee that they will obtain agreement from colleagues on their own ideas. In addition, such ideas are often undertaken by trial and error and employees are supposed to learn from failure, which is often unacceptable in the main business. However, by implementing activities in situations other than the main business, it is expected to generate a synergistic effect of social contribution and employee satisfaction improvement. Against this background, Kizuna Activities have been implemented.

Mitsubishi Heavy Industries Group has several forms of activities to fulfil social responsibility. Among them, there are two types of activities that both make a social contribution and increase employee satisfaction—formal activities and informal activities. Formal activities are activities led by the company mainly at the factory level, such as community cleaning, tree planting, charity concerts for social contribution, long distance relay races and athletic meets, aiming at improving employee satisfaction. These activities are regarded as 'places' for fostering a sense of unity and communication between employees working in the same workplace, and have been implemented as top-down and workplace-only activities.

Meanwhile, informal activities do not rely on the company's support but instead, on the independence of employees. In short, employees propose themes by themselves, and gather supporting members (across departments) who have a common awareness of the issue. Thus, these are bottom-up and cross-organisational activities organised and implemented by employees themselves. The theme can be anything that is not directly related to the main business but ultimately improves the company as a whole. Kizuna Activities belong to the latter category, and originally started in 2006 at the former Engine Business Unit of Mitsubishi Heavy Industries, with four themes, involving about 30 people.

By increasing employee satisfaction, these activities not only aim to improve the quality of work but also enhance individual competency by working spontaneously and collaboratively. At the same time, attention is also paid to gaining the trust of the society and community. These informal activities have made significant progress under the direction by Takio Nishizuma, who has served as an executive officer of Mitsubishi Heavy Industries and as Vice President of Mitsubishi Hitachi Power Systems. These projects are currently carried out by ten members of a coordinating group, led by Toshiya Ejima, Deputy General Manager of the Sales Division of Mitsubishi Hitachi Power Systems, instead of a traditional CSR department. With the establishment of Mitsubishi Hitachi Power Systems, these activities were renamed as Kizuna Activities in 2014, but the scope of the activities itself has not changed significantly.

Kizuna Activities are a generic term for the social activities of Mitsubishi Heavy Industries Group, in which employees propose themes that contribute to society and increase employee satisfaction, and supporting members who agree with the proposal gather together across departments during non-business hours.[1] The activity name is derived from the direct meaning of 'Kizuna' (i.e. bonds or ties) and the indirect (unique) meaning of 'kyoukara, *zutto, nakama' (i.e., from today, always friends). The company is involved only in: (1) calling for themes that lead to 'social contribution and employee satisfaction' that allows employees to work as a team, (2) calling for supporting members who want to work together to realise the theme across divisions, and (3) providing a framework in which the theme proposer and supporting members gather and work outside of business hours for one year to realise the theme (it is possible to continue for several years).

In other words, based on the basic concepts of 'spontaneity' and 'collaboration,' employees themselves propose a theme that contributes to the society and increases employee satisfaction, and subsequently gather supporting members. The work in this direction is performed outside of working hours, and all the duties are left to the employees. Depending on the theme, activities during working hours may be permitted, and a certain amount of budget can be allocated, but there is no reward even if results are achieved. As of March 2018, 27 activities have been carried out, such as 'science experiment workshops', 'photo cleaning project', 'support to fight hunger in developing countries', and 'elementary school soccer tournament'. The specific contents of these activities are reported at the annual meetings.

In Kizuna Activities, emphasis is given on its principle that the proposal of themes, the participation of supporting members, and the way to proceed with the activities are independent and autonomous, not forced by anyone. Moreover, members of the activity are able to work together and communicate by removing all barriers such as segregation by department, occupation, job title, age and gender, and by forming a bright and free place where everyone can talk freely and openly. Above all, emphasis is especially placed on horizontal connections by removing all barriers, because it is expected that this will increase employee satisfaction further by promoting mutual understanding between employees and giving each other good stimulation.

[1] Ejima, T. (2018) Off-the-Job Initiatives Driven by Employees' Autonomy and Collaboration (Kizuna Activities), *Journal of Kanagawa Policy Research and University Collaboration*, No. 12, pp. 146–149 (in Japanese).

Mitsubishi Heavy Industries Group expects that the following effects will result from the Kizuna Activities:

(1) Increasing employee satisfaction in addition to contributing to the society by having employees engage in social activities on their own,
(2) Improving the quality of work by increasing employee satisfaction via an increase in motivation and professionalism,
(3) Increasing the satisfaction of the society and customers by providing a higher quality of products and services via a higher quality of work, and.
(4) Making the company sustainable by improving business performance through an increase in social and customer satisfaction and at the same time, encouraging the growth of employees through process-oriented activities.

Mitsubishi Heavy Industries Group has been conducting such activities for a long time and has realised that employees have been able to communicate efficiently and create a sense of unity as an organisation. In addition, Mitsubishi Hitachi Power Systems was established by merging from two companies belonging to different 'parent companies', which has required more balanced communication between employees than ever before; thus, it can be said that the importance of Kizuna Activities is increasing. In the next section, we will discuss the specific examples of Kizuna Activities.

8.3 Practices of Kizuna Activities

8.3.1 Science Experiment Workshops

The science experiment workshops are undertaken to inspire dreams and hopes in children (who will be responsible for the future) by communicating, learning, and enjoying together during the science experiments. Here, the recent problem of elementary school students drifting away from science is being addressed. The aim of the workshops is to increase children's (mainly elementary school students) interest in science by making them experience the joy of science experiments and the challenges in producing electricity by way of experiments—for instance, the 'fruit battery experiments'. For this purpose, the project team visits elementary schools all over Japan. These science experiment workshops have always been well received, and some elementary schools often request their revisit (Fig. 8.1).

The science experiment workshops have been implemented since 2014. However, this activity has its roots in a personal activity by Hiroshi Ishizaka, the project leader of the Environmental Plant Division of Mitsubishi Hitachi Power Systems. As of 2018, 12 project members from Yokohama, Kobe, Takasago, Kure, and Nagasaki have joined this activity. Every five or six members usually deliver the science experiment workshops at a pace of about five times a year. The project team plans to increase the number of these workshops.

Fig. 8.1 Science experiment workshops

However, since the workshops are a non-business activity, they are essentially held during the weekends. The project team does not have a specific space for the activity, and although the project members can communicate with each other by telephone or email, they can only meet each other at the venues. The number of students present fluctuates depending on the class and the grade; there are usually dozens of students and sometimes nearly 100 at the most for some popular activities. In addition to elementary schools, the project team sometimes visits the recreation facilities of Mitsubishi Heavy Industries Group and conducts these workshops for employees' children as summer vacation events.

The characteristic of this activity is that all members, including those with a background in humanities as well as sciences, act as lecturers (at least once) in the science experiment workshops. However, in these workshops, it is necessary to provide a lucid explanation to elementary school students and answer unexpected questions from them. As such, members who do not specialise in science and those who have no experience in public speaking have been very reluctant to undertake this task. Therefore, only project members with a science background, including Ishizaka, served as lecturers in the early days. However, as the project members continued the project, they eventually changed their mind and proactively supported the project, including taking on the role of lecturers.

This applies to all the Kizuna Activities, and the fact that the lateral connection between employees has become stronger is related to the enhancement of the activities. These activities provide a valuable opportunity to deepen mutual understanding among employees who have little contact with each other as they are limited by their specific work. This is also true for those from Mitsubishi and Hitachi who were competitors before the merger and had difficulty in getting acquainted with each other.

In other words, although people with high motivation have participated in this activity, if the lateral connection can become stronger, they can affect and enhance each other's motivation further. This leads to the types of motivation characterised by the sentiments—'let's try it', 'let's challenge even difficult things', and 'let's make a better class'. As a result, to undertake the role of a lecturer, they actively take measures such as referring to the classes of other lecturers and holding a meeting to acquire the necessary knowledge.

Furthermore, a lot of stimulation and awareness is derived from the children participating in the science experiment workshops. This is evident from the comments of the project members: 'I feel my mind refreshed when I see children working hard' and 'I am deeply touched by the purity of children'. Moreover, owing to the thank-you letters from the children who participated, all the project members gradually feel more motivated to conduct these workshops because they realise that this activity is valuable. In fact, some project members said, 'I feel more comfortable being a lecturer', and 'I feel the significance of contributing to society'. In this way, witnessing direct reactions from children brings joy and self-confidence, which in turn helps increase motivation. This is because, as some project member said, 'I have never thought to be stimulated by the children', it is only from these activities that employees feel something special emanating from the purity of the children.

In this way, the science experiment workshops increase the project members' motivation through connections with peers (i.e. horizontal relationships; which are difficult to achieve in the main business) and by interacting with the children. The project members commented—'I come to love science because of this activity'; 'I can work hard because I can do "Kizuna Activities" after the job'; and 'I have felt that hardships are no longer hardship'—which show that these workshops increase employees' motivation. These effects are obtained only by employees who work independently while communicating with each other.

In addition, these science experiment workshops have gained good reputation from children and their parents, which shows that increasing employees' motivation can also have a positive effect on social contributions of the company. The increase in employee satisfaction resulting from this activity is the original purpose of the Kizuna Activities, and is expected to have an indirect impact on the main business. Therefore, the science experiment workshops are a good example of social contribution activities that employees independently carry out and can have a positive effect not only on social contribution but also on the main business.

8.3.2 *Photo Cleaning Project*

The photo cleaning project has been implemented since August 2011 by a project team that aims to clean and repair photos and albums lost or damaged in the tsunami caused by the Great East Japan Earthquake that occurred in March 2011, and return them to their original owners. After completing the project in about six years, it has now been expanded to include damaged photos in various areas of Japan. In the six years up to 2017, a total of 1,500 photo cleaning activities have been carried out, with a total of 15,000 participants. As a result, two million photos have been cleaned and repaired, and they were returned to their original owners (i.e. the person themselves, their families, or their stakeholders). Accordingly, the photo cleaning project has been greatly appreciated by residents in the devastated areas. One of the features of this project is that it is a collaborative activity involving outside supporters such as local residents and volunteers (Fig. 8.2).

The photo cleaning project began in July 2011, four months after the earthquake. It was started on an individual level by Makiko Takenaka from the Mitsubishi Hitachi Power Systems Sales Division, the first project leader who participated in a volunteer activity for photo cleaning in Yamada-cho, Iwate Prefecture. After the earthquake, a large number of photos and albums of unknown ownership that were washed away by the tsunami were collected. However, it was necessary to clean and repair them first because it took time to find the owners but the photos eroded by the sea would lose their original shape with time going on.

Takenaka witnessed the enormous damage and felt that continuous volunteer activities were necessary. She was thinking about what she could do since it was difficult to visit the devastated areas frequently, and it was not a problem that can be tackled solely on her own. At that time, Takenaka immediately applied (to the

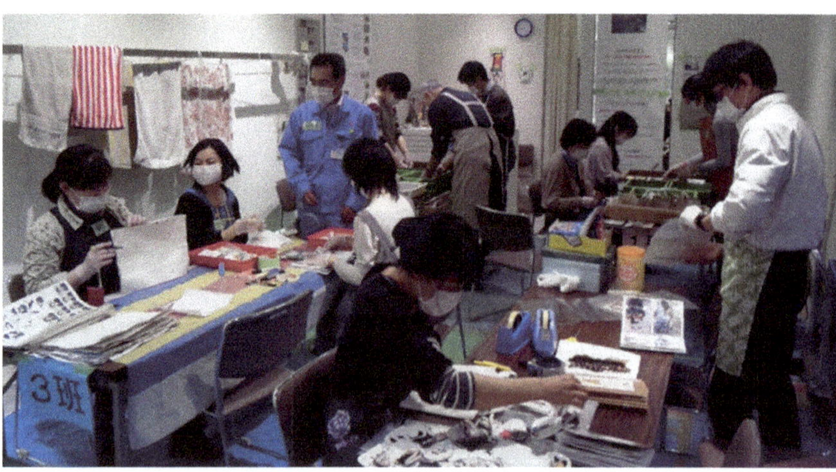

Fig. 8.2 Photo cleaning project scene

company) for a 'photo cleaning project' because she thought that photo cleaning was an activity that could support the devastated areas without the need of on-site visits, and many supporters could gather in Yokohama where the company was located.

This application was approved immediately, and the first round of activities began in mid-August. The photo cleaning project was able to start in such a short period because the project gained full cooperation from a company with knowledge and techniques on cleaning and repairing photos. Besides, it also benefited from being able to renting the activity venue on the ground floor of the MHI Yokohama Building (where the headquarters of Mitsubishi Hitachi Power Systems are located) free of charge. Despite the short preparation period, there were many applications when supporters were recruited. By the end of September, a total of 638 people, including 10 core members from inside and outside the company, had participated in the activity. These people gathered not only because of internal notices, the spread of information through posters and blogs, and recommendations from some organisations that implemented similar activities, but also due to the introduction of this project by the media. In addition, some people happened to join in the activities upon seeing them take place in the rented venue.

During the peak period, activities for the photo cleaning project were held at three locations, the MHI Yokohama Building, the Kanazawa Plant (in Yokohama), and the MHI Building (in Shinagawa, Tokyo), where the Mitsubishi Heavy Industries Tokyo Head Office is located, sometimes with more than 50 participants per event. In addition, since the photos immersed in seawater was eroded quickly, activities were carried out every day in the early days of the project. Thanks to such activities, the number of damaged photos that needed to be cleaned and repaired was considerably reduced, and the activities settled down accordingly. As a result, the activities for the photo cleaning project are currently carried out irregularly at a pace of two or three times a month in the meeting room of MHI Yokohama Building.

The photo cleaning project is one of the long-standing Kizuna Activities. One of the major driving forces was the cooperation of external supporters. In fact, the internal project members of the company have often said that 'this project cannot be continued without the cooperation of external supporters, such as local residents and volunteers'. The external supporters helped a lot, not only in terms of the manpower they provided but also concerning their high motivation. Such horizontal connections beyond employees have provided a better stimulus than working only with internal project members. However, it was not easy for the leaders to manage a group with members of different characteristics, including external supporters.

The first leader, Takenaka, and the current leader, Mariko Miyazaki of Mitsubishi Hitachi Power Systems Power & Energy Solutions Business Division, mentioned that it was difficult to manage members with different motivations and communicate with external supporters. This shows that Takenaka and Miyazaki realised the difficulty in conducting a different type of organisational management that they had never experienced in their main business. However, experiencing such difficulties is very helpful in terms of human resource development, and it is expected that such experiences will be useful in the main business in the future.

Meanwhile, some external supporters of the project commented, 'we are grateful for having been provided a place where we can participate volunteer activities.' This shows that while the cooperation of external supporters has been indispensable for the photo cleaning project, for external supporters, participation in the project also has met their need. In other words, unintentionally, the photo cleaning project has fulfilled its social responsibilities not only for those in the devastated areas, but also for those who have such a need of volunteer work. In fact, feedback on the company is given in the form of evaluations and reliability improvements of Mitsubishi Heavy Industries Group, and the internal project members felt that 'we are highly evaluated more than we think'. In other words, although the photo cleaning project was originally aimed at recovering from the earthquake, this project actually had more potential effect than originally considered.

Another major driving force was the company's flexible response to this project. The internal project members actually recognised this, and they especially appreciated the company's attitude of respecting and approving employees' willingness and efforts to contribute to the recovery from the earthquake, as well as being open to people outside the company. These have transformed the image of the company in a good way and impressed internal project members. For example, some internal project members commented, 'The company's support to this activity is stronger than I have ever expected even though it is not an activity for the company, which makes me feel that I have to do something to return the favour', and 'I couldn't feel very close to the company because of its stiff image, but thanks to this project, I feel closer to the company. I began to think afresh about the company and came to love it'. Thus, the company's flexible response to this project has improved employee satisfaction and their devotion to the company, which is expected to have a positive impact on the main business as well.

As described above, while the cooperation of external supporters and the flexible responses from the company are the driving forces of the photo cleaning project, in the process, the employees have gained a new perspective on the company and its main business. In terms of increasing employee satisfaction, the sense of fulfilment is observed from comments such as 'I changed my outlook on life. I have been affected so much that I feel like that I was totally changed', 'I am grateful to participate volunteer activities because my relatives live in the devastated area', and 'We have been able to contact and connect with various people inside and outside the company'. However, not only these feelings of satisfaction, but also this new awareness is very important from the perspective of human resource development. These effects can be obtained only after employees themselves took the initiative in social contribution activities that were not directly related to their main business. In other words, the key to the success of the photo cleaning project as a social contribution and human resource development activity seems to be the fact that while thinking about the devastated area, employees can feel 'I like myself', 'I like my friends' and 'I love my company', which are difficult to realise through the main business.

8.4 Characteristic of Emergent Responsible Management: Pursuit of Responsibility Through the Organisation

In the Kizuna Activities carried out by Mitsubishi Heavy Industries Group to contribute to society and increase employee satisfaction, employees themselves propose themes and take actions together with supporting members with a common awareness of the problem independently gathered across departments, without limiting the responsibilities of the company. Thus, Kizuna Activities are regarded as one of the practices of emergent responsible management in terms of pursuing infinite responsibility and the spontaneity of participants. In particular, it is a type that respects the spontaneity of employees beyond the scope of regular work. This trend can be seen particularly from the examples introduced above, because they were initiated from personal activities of employees.

Kizuna Activities are informal activities that are implemented beyond the scope of the main business, which also reflect and make full use of the characteristics of Mitsubishi Heavy Industries Group. The projects have had significant social impacts not only by taking advantage of Mitsubishi Heavy Industries Group's technological know-how, but also by leveraging the company's network, even if these activities have little relation to its technological know-how. Moreover, as seen in the photo cleaning project, the expansion of network in the society allowed activities to be further promoted. Thus, the characteristics of the philosopher Iris Marion Young's responsibilities (introduced in Chap. 3) as a social connection model are also confirmed by the Kizuna Activities.

Besides, although the Kizuna Activities were originally started to increase employee satisfaction, it is important to note that while actually fulfilling social responsibilities, employee satisfaction was improved, leading to human resource development and a sense of organisational unity. This is an important characteristic of this activity. In emergent responsible management, fulfilling the responsibility is expected to create value. However, a characteristic of the Kizuna Activities is that these activities not only create the value by solving social issues but also benefit the company itself. Since the Kizuna Activities are process-oriented activities that are implemented beyond the scope of the main business, the higher the degree of freedom of employees in the activity, the more likely the effects will be obtained.

Therefore, the Kizuna Activities can be understood as a mechanism by which a company, as an organisation, supports individual employee to realise their responsibility and take action. The examples from the other four companies introduced in this book are part of the employees' regular work, although these are somehow independent from the main business. In contrast, the 'Kizuzuna Activities' are strongly related to employees' volunteer activities, which are beyond the scope of their main business. However, the fact that the company supports these activities demonstrates that it is aware of its responsibility as an organisation with significant resources. The Kizuna Activities could never be realised if the company regards them as the individuals' own ideas and does not support them. Thus, companies that have far more resources than individuals are considered to have responsibility to respond to such needs. With these activities, Mitsubishi Heavy Industries Group fulfil its responsibility not as an economic organisation but as an entity with human resource and technical competence, and in that sense, such initiative can be considered the archetype of emergent responsible management.

To conduct such activities, it is important to have a system in which activities can be continued to solve social issues as long as employees have a strong will. The increase in employee satisfaction resulting from the Kizuna Activities guarantees this, and at the same time it indicates that emergent responsible management can also have a positive effect on the main business. Not only the fact that there are many projects (such as photo cleaning projects) that have been continued for a long time, but also growing interest in Kizuna Activities within the company support this view. This example provides important insights on how to fulfil CSR in the future.

Chapter 9
Design of Emergent Responsible Management

Hirotsugu Kitada and Katsuhiko Kokubu

Abstract Based on cases in previous chapters, this chapter aims to develop the corresponding organisational design to encourage the continued practice of emergent responsible management in companies. Firstly, we have categorised the previous cases into three different types, i.e. corporate philosophy-driven type, social problem-oriented type and spontaneity-oriented type. In addressing how the activities in these companies have been carried out beyond the traditional framework of corporate management, this chapter sheds light on the design of emergent responsible management from the viewpoint of exploration and exploitation of knowledge based on organisational ambidexterity. In addition, we examine how we can make full use of the management resources that have been accumulated through exploitation, without being isolated in the organisation, and discuss how to balance social contribution activities and the business. By conducting emergent responsible management, various links are created between stakeholders and management resources, and value is created both for society and the organisation. The design of the organisation for this purpose not only promotes activities but also changes the boundaries of the organisation.

9.1 Types of Emergent Responsible Management

We introduced the cases of five companies from Chap. 4 to 8 as examples of emergent responsible management. Each one is unique and varies in content, and we have categorised them into the following three types. Cases based on the corporate philosophy, such as those of OMRON and Bridgestone, are classified as *corporate philosophy-driven.* The cases of Marui Group and Yahoo Japan are categorised as *social problem-oriented* because they mainly aim to solve social issues. Mitsubishi Heavy Industry Group's activities are voluntary activities of employees, which have the farthest relationship with its main business among the five cased; thus, it is classified as *spontaneity-oriented.*

The original version of this chapter was revised: Belated corrections received in Chapters 1, 2, 9 and 11 have been updated. The correction to this chapter is available at https://doi.org/10.1007/978-981-19-0416-5_13

K. Kokubu et al., *Emergent Responsible Management*, Kobe University Monograph Series in Social Science Research, https://doi.org/10.1007/978-981-19-0416-5_9

However, all of the practices conducted by these five companies share three elements. Firstly, not only Marui Group and Yahoo Japan, but also the OMRON, Bridgestone, and Mitsubishi Heavy Industries Group are challenging social issues. Furthermore, without a firm corporate philosophy, no projects of any company could continue. Lastly, spontaneity is also a basis of all these companies' projects. Therefore, the above-mentioned classification merely indicates the predominant feature of these cases. It is important to understand the characteristics of each case and consider what is necessary for the design of emergent responsible management. For this purpose, we will summarise the cases of these five companies before discussing the design.

OMRON, under the strong leadership of Yoshihito Yamada as the president, conducts TOGA to realise the corporate philosophy 'to improve lives and contribute to a better society.' By undertaking this project, the company makes it possible to take on those projects that may be not so attractive in terms of profitability but make strong social contribution. The corporate philosophy is generally an abstract idea, and in the case of OMRON, no specific activities are suggested either. However, over 30,000 projects have been implemented based on that abstract philosophy. The reason why this initiative is so successful is that the top management including Yamada understands the significance of the corporate philosophy and gives warm encouragement to employees who have worked hard, which leads them to exert more efforts on its practice. Emergent responsible management can be well implemented through such interaction between employees and top management.

Bridgestone has been developing activities with the new concept, *Our Way to Serve*, which reflects the mission of the corporate philosophy, 'Serving Society with Superior Quality', and encourages employees to contribute to society. Through the Bridgestone Global Awards, various activities that are voluntarily undertaken by employees worldwide are linked to the global management system. In this way, Bridgestone succeeded in constructing a flexible management system for CSR by taking advantage of the initiative of each site. *Our Way to Serve* clarifies the areas of activity, i.e. 'Mobility', 'People', and 'Environment', and it leaves considerable freedom for diverse individual activities. This suggests that in emergent responsible management it is important not only to support individual spontaneous activities, but also to link those activities to the company's overall management system.

Under the strong leadership of Hiroshi Aoi as the president, Marui Group, whose case is classified as a *social problem-oriented type*, has launched 'co-creation (sustainability) management' and adopted the concept of *inclusion* to achieve this. One of its important initiatives is an 'official group project team' in which employees can voluntarily participate. Marui Group organises these teams to address several key social issues. These topics are in line with the current global social situation including Japan.

Aoi regards sustainability initiatives as 'what everyone wants to do', and places emphasis on creating an environment that fully embraces employees' spontaneity. The members of the official group project teams are regularly given time and provided a place independent from normal work so that they can concentrate on the project. In addition, an environment that facilitates cooperation within the organisation is created by allocating senior managers as supporters. Through these initiatives, Marui Group encourages employees' spontaneity and consequently brings about many emergent activities.

Yahoo Japan has been working on the earthquake recovery projects in Tohoku region which is Japan's biggest social issue in recent years. Here, the corporate philosophy works as an action guideline with the employees' independence emphasised, thus speedy decision-making at the workplace has been conducted and the company generates positive social impact on the region. One of the characteristics of Yahoo Japan's case is that it involves local stakeholders, mainly with activities of the Ishinomaki Base. There are almost no specific instructions on the operation of daily work, which are conducted independently by employees. Yahoo Japan's organisational culture allows a flexible business process where without relying on specific instructions from their superior, employees are permitted to implement the project first and correct it later if it does not work. This is one way of designing emergent responsible management to cultivate the independence of employees.

The case of Mitsubishi Heavy Industries Group, which is classified as *spontaneity-oriented type*, has less involvement with its main business than the other four companies. Although the other four company's cases do not only focus on gains, they nevertheless expect positive effects on their core business over the medium to long term. In the case of Mitsubishi Heavy Industries Group, they indirectly assume the activities to have an effect on the company by increasing employee satisfaction, but not expect any direct effect on the main business explicitly.

However, activities that contribute to society using the internal network of such a large company provide an opportunity for employees to 'be conscious' of their responsibility. In the Kizuna Activities, it is possible to work independently and autonomously without being forced by anyone, including developing themes, recruiting members, and proceeding with the activities. This is designed to promote solidarity and communication by removing various barriers in the organisation such as segregation by department, occupation, job title, age and gender, and create a bright and free place where the members can talk with each other freely. The company is able to improve employee satisfaction and the quality of work by contributing to society, and also enhances organisational capabilities through the employees' spontaneous behaviour and collaborative experience.

As a common feature of these cases, the management style that promotes the spontaneity of employees and their consciousness of social responsibility has created diverse connections among project members, other organisation members, and external stakeholders. These connections create a variety of interactive relationships within and outside the organisation and potentially generate emergent value. In each case, to create value from the spontaneous efforts of employees, the companies work out to devise appropriate ways to organise the project. In this chapter, we consider this design issue of emergent responsible management from the viewpoint of *exploration* and *exploitation* of knowledge. In the next section, we will summarise the meaning of value creation through emergent responsible management first.

9.2 Value Creation Through Emergent Responsible Management

The concept of emergence[1] has been used in fields such as sociology and organisational theory to capture the effects of interaction between individuals. Especially in the field of management studies, it has contributed to the understanding of value creation and innovation by focusing on the interaction between actors. As discussed in Chap. 3, Kokuryo defines the concept of 'emergence' as follows. The two points in the definition are important.

> 'A situation in which many players are combining diverse resources and creating unexpected new values one after another while doing their own jobs without assuming a specific consequence in advance'.[2]

The first point is that 'without assuming a specific consequence in advance'. Clearly setting strategies and targets in advance with management indicators is effective in terms of integrating different departments of the organisation and improving overall motivation in order to operate the organisation efficiently. This approach was effective in the mass-production business model of the twentieth century. However, if we continue to rely only on this approach, it will be difficult to keep up with recent changes in ways of communication due to innovative technology. Setting goals to be achieved also restricts employees' behaviour, thereby limiting the scope for creating new things. Emergent management focuses on promoting activities by designing activities and interactive processes, rather than managing the organisation by setting goals such as KPIs in advance.

---

[1] As mentioned in Chap. 3, emergence is originally a term from natural science, and the interaction of the constituents of the whole causes the emergence of unexpected characteristics from individual characteristics. This means that such interactions are repeated. Water is composed of oxygen and hydrogen molecules, but the properties of water cannot be reduced to those of oxygen and hydrogen molecules. A new property, water, is created by combining oxygen molecules and hydrogen molecules.

[2] Kokuryo, J. and Platform Design Lab (2011) *Emergency Management Platform: Creating an Information Infrastructure for Collaboration*, Nikkei Publishing Inc., p. 2 (in Japanese).

It is necessary to consider the second point, 'combining diverse resources', when designing the place of such activities and the process of interaction. Management studies have attempted to capture the process of creativity and innovation as a way of coupling. If there are many types of management resources that can be used to create connections, various new combinations are expected. Organisations can manage connections within and across departments through brainstorming and projects. They can also manage connections with various actors outside the organisation through customer interfaces and open architecture. Any site or communication process is designed for the diversity of connections.

By linking this concept of emergence to infinite responsibility, this book proposes a management model in which on-site employees can work on their own initiative. Emergent responsible management is a process in which employees repeatedly interact with stakeholders inside and outside the organisation to search for social responsibility related initiatives to work on, creating new ideas and connections with society that could not have been expected in conventional CSR. This would help address social issues that have often been overlooked, and would eventually lead to processes that create new value for companies.

The relationship between value creation and responsibility linked by the concept of emergence can also be understood as the interaction between limited rationality and the pursuit of infinite responsibility. James March and Herbert Simon,[3] who set up the foundation for innovation and organisational learning, point out that human cognition is limited. Therefore, even if there are countless options, only those that can be recognised are considered as options, and only limited rationality can be exhibited in the decision-making process. To overcome this, the emphasis is on the process of exploring new options beyond what is known.

Meanwhile, as explained in Chap. 2, while the society has become more complex, people tend to limit their responsibility to avoid risks, which makes it difficult to recognise a myriad of available options. It narrows the cognitive scope of organisation members and makes it difficult to see their relationship with society. The solution is to apply infinite responsibility. Approaching the world with an attitude that considers everything as one's own responsibility mitigates these cognitive limitations. Therefore, emergent responsible management should not be shaped by institutions and organisational structures but naturally appears through practice. Previous studies of organisational learning and innovation have attempted to clarify the process of exploring new options to overcome cognitive limitations and remove factors that hinder them. We propose a new approach to overcoming limited rationality by transforming a limited recognition of responsibility to an infinite recognition. Based on these discussions, this chapter will consider the management mechanism that supports emergent responsible management with the idea of the *exploration* and *exploitation* of knowledge. For this purpose, we need to take two points below into account.

[3] March, J. G. and Simon, H. (1993) *Organizations* (Second Edition), John Willy & Sons.

First, we need to consider the relationship between the main businesses and social contribution efforts. Practising emergent responsible management has the potential to create new value by linking social issues with the management resources in the company. Management of the main business and efforts for social contribution should not be regarded as suppressing or contradicting each other. Rather, we need to think about how we can adjust that relationship.

Second, we should consider how management can promote *exploration* through emergent responsible management and discuss how to design organisation by considering the employees' roles, the way of sharing the issues, and internal motivation with reference to the examples presented in this book.

9.3 Exploration and Exploitation of Knowledge

In the five cases presented in this book, the participants have found a good balance between finding new issues and mobilising internal resources to resolve them. The former is a process of recognising issues that have not been regarded as one's own responsibility before. The latter is about mobilising resources, including know-how and personnel skills cultivated within the company, to solve such issues.

With reference to organisational ambidexterity,[4] we examine how to design an organisation to balance these two aspects. Organisational ambidexterity is a framework for managing knowledge creation through exploration and exploitation. The idea is to balance *exploration* for finding new ideas with *exploitation* for developing businesses based on existing management resources.

Addressing global issues such as environmental and social problems is also an opportunity for employees to become aware of the relationship between the company and society, which cannot be recognised in their ordinary business activities. Therefore, in emergent responsible management, an employee's spontaneous attempt to find a new link between himself/herself and the society functions as an exploration process that expands the employee's perspective into a new world. Furthermore, by using what they find, exploitation of the organisation will be strengthened.

As mentioned in Chap. 6, Marui Group held a suit-fitting event for transgender people as an LGBT-related initiative. In dealing with LGBT customers that have difficulty in choosing a suit, sales clerks come to understand that customer needs are diverse and they need to change the way to provide customer service. The structure of the sales floor was changed to provide a wide range of products that accommodate everyone, including LGBTs. For example, Men's shoes ranged in size from 22.5 to 30 cm, thus previously unrecognised customer segments were newly targeted.

---

[4] This chapter refers to Iriyama, S. (2015) *Aiming for 'Ambidextrousness' Is the Essence of Innovation*, Diamond Company (in Japanese).

Exploration activities to gain such new perspectives often end with one-off activities or turn to be isolated from the organisation as a special case. However, by preventing such isolation and balancing this with existing management resources, new ideas can be expected to bring about greater effects. The key to organisational design is to create a link between the new knowledge gained from addressing social issues and the management of know-how and networks that companies have accumulated in their usual business activities.

To challenge social issues is to create value with a new connection between outside and inside the company. The approach of *outside-in*,[5] which is emphasised when introducing the SDGs into a company, can also be regarded as a process of incorporating the thinking of stakeholders outside the organisation. This can be understood as an effort to foster interaction between actors inside and outside the organisation, which has the same structure with the act of seeking one's responsibility to others.

As discussed above, the concepts of exploration and exploitation of knowledge can be perfectly used to describe the organisational design in emergent responsible management. Regarding the balance between exploration and exploitation of knowledge, Charles O'Reilly and Michael Tushman[6] make emphasis on two aspects based on the USA Today case. Firstly, aiming for the exploration of knowledge this company set up an organisation to seek new business and it is important that this organisation is simultaneously independent from other departments. Secondly, they point out that it is critical for the management to encourage the integration and communication of the new organisation and existing departments to share knowledge and resources without isolating them. The emergent responsible management initiatives of the case firms can also be understood as a process of interaction and integration between project-based initiatives and existing departments. Independence of the new organisation is required to acquire new knowledge, but it is impossible to make use of that knowledge in isolation.

Regarding independence of the organisation for exploration, in the case firms, it is common that the emergent teams are somewhat spatially and temporally independent from normal operations. For example, Yahoo Japan's Ishinomaki Base is geographically remote from its headquarter; thus, its members could find problems by themselves and freely explore ways to solve them. The activities began with the aim for the recovery of the Tohoku region, and then expanded into resolving issues faced by local communities. Ishinomaki base has been recognised by the headquarters as a place for pilot projects, thus setting goals for activities with a high degree of freedom is allowed.

---

[5] For more detailed explanation, see Chap. 11.

[6] O'Reilly, C. and Tushman, M. (2004) The Ambidextrous Organization, *Harvard Business Review*, April, pp. 74–81.

Some of the staff at Ishinomaki Base also serve as directors and staff at Fisherman Japan. This allows them to understand the characteristics of the fishery and the surrounding community, which they do not have the chance to get to know in the Tokyo office. The design of such activities allows new knowledge to be incorporated into the network of their activities, and such new knowledge will improve the approach to the problem. In a seafood supply chain, there are often conflicts of interest between fishermen and wholesalers, as well as retail outlets. To promote regional development in marine resources, it is necessary to find clues to solutions by understanding local situation.

As one method of exploration of knowledge, relocating human resources outside the company has been often employed by Japanese companies. In the case of Yahoo Japan, the understanding of the social issues of the employees there has been more comprehensive and in-depth by being dispatch to Fisherman Japan. On the other hand, the activities of Ishinomaki Base are not isolated from the headquarters. In addition to regular meetings and reporting, a network has been established with the headquarters through formal and informal interactions. The 'Tour de Tohoku', and 'Yale market', which were launched at Ishinomaki Base, have been taken over by the head office. Ishinomaki Base also serves as a place for pilot project and new attempt, influencing, for example, the design of the open space at the headquarters. The links are also spreading outside the organisation, and these interactions benefit stakeholders. Local people who engage in the activities, like those from Fisherman Japan, tend to lack management skills and social networks, but the staff from Yahoo Japan compensate for this deficiency.

Marui Group develops 'official group project teams' in which employees can voluntarily apply for and participate in activities from areas of interest such as diversity, health management, and sustainability. Being an 'official group project team' guarantees the independence of its activities in two respects. One is that the team is separated temporally and spatially and is independent of ordinary work. For example, once a month, the members will gather as a team to hold discussions or attend study sessions by external lecturers for certain theme, away from regular work. The other is that senior managers will provide support for an environment in which younger members can work independently from their regular work. The senior managers involved in an 'official group project team' are responsible for coordinating the relationship between the project members and their superiors to guarantee that the members are able to focus on the project.

Realising organisational ambidexterity through the balance between exploration and exploitation is also a process of adjusting projects that seek for new things to be successfully integrated without being isolated from existing organisations. With regard to the cases in this book, top management and senior managers encourage communication and integration by coordinating the organisational structure for both emergent and existing activities. In the case of Marui Group, the middle management's involvement in the 'official group project team' promoted their understanding of the activities. Many managers gained a deeper understanding through the experience as the support members and became more sympathetic to the activities undertaken by the younger members. In addition, health management activities for senior managers have been implemented as a program for resilience. The deepening of the managers' understanding has created an environment that facilitates the integration of ideas conceived by young members of the 'official group project team' into organisational activities.

Bridgestone's top management tries to incorporate the concept, *Our Way to Serve,* into its organisational culture by authorising employees' voluntary social contributions through the Bridgestone Global Awards. The management system is designed in a way that *Our Way to Serve* initiatives are reported to management on a regular basis, and the issues are shared at group level.

The organisational structure of emergent responsible management in the cases is designed to support employees' engagement. Emergent activities facilitate exploration of social issues that have not been recognised in conventional organisational activities, and the knowledge-exploration process works effectively for the organisation. On the other hand, these activities are isolated from the existing business activities, but have been integrated into the normal organisation, with the understanding of the management and a shared recognition of its importance within the company. In the case companies, management attempts to balance exploration (the search for knowledge) and exploitation (the deepening of knowledge) by designing an organisational structure that uses existing management resources to solve newly identified social problems.

The most important process in emergent responsible management is, clearly, recognising social issues and taking actions accordingly. However, entrusting the resolution of social issues to the discretion of employees is costly both in terms of time and personnel. Furthermore, it is often difficult to know what value will be created from an activity until it is implemented. Even in the context of innovation and creativity, the process of exploration to create something new can succeed or fail and is highly uncertain and costly. For this reason, organisations are inclined to get slack at searching for knowledge or tend to focus on exploitation with the low uncertainty of such activities. However, if that happens, organisations will not be able to fulfil their infinite responsibility. Therefore, to promote emergent responsible management, it is necessary to design a place that encourages interaction between internal members and external stakeholders as a process of exploration.

The PDCA cycle is often adopted in the design of sustainability management systems, such as the *SDG Compass*, the guide for business action on the SDGs, and ISO 14001, an international standard for environmental management systems. However, as the definition of emergence includes 'without assuming any particular consequence in advance,' the process of knowledge creation, such as exploration, is incompatible with the style of setting goals in advance and controlling them with KPIs. Especially, mechanisms to enhance motivation through incentive systems can even be bad for the performance of emergent activities.

Therefore, for exploration, it is necessary to consider an approach different from the PDCA cycle. While the specific process is explained in Chap. 10, here, we discuss the way to design a place to explore responsibility for social issues through interaction with stakeholders. We present three important points: the roles of participants, sharing of the issues (the basis of communication), and the desires of the participants (internal motivation).[7]

9.4 Designing a Place to Explore Responsibility

9.4.1 The Role of Participants

Members who participate in emergent responsible management serve as the link between the organisation and external stakeholders. By participating in the project, employees become aware of a role different from what is assigned in their normal work. However, if they try to contribute voluntarily to society individually, they are not able to make full use of the resources of the company to increase the impact. In the cases introduced in this book, these employees are also conscious of practising their responsibility to society as part of a corporate project that is consistent with the organisation's guiding principle. In this sense, emergent responsible management is different from a pure volunteer activity by an individual, as it is performed as part of the organisational activities, even though the individual determines the activity.

In the case companies, the application of guiding principles to activities differed. They all conducted the activities based on the corporate philosophy, but the way to communicate their philosophy to employees differed. In Yahoo Japan, where the degree of freedom is the highest, under the company's slogan 'Problem-solving engine', the person in charge is allowed to seek out the problem by himself/herself and develops activities to solve it. For instance, initially, an office was opened in Ishinomaki to support the earthquake recovery, and at present, it is targeted for regional development centred on fisheries. They have flexibility in choosing their targets. In OMRON's projects aiming for realising corporate philosophy, issues to be addressed are not clearly specified. In this sense, the freedom of activities is the same as those in Yahoo Japan. Bridgestone, on the other hand, has given a specific direction in its initiative, *Our Way to Serve,* by providing particular areas to pursue—mobility, people, and environment. Marui Group has the clearest direction of activities, and Aoi has shown specific ideas for each theme, which are strongly

[7] For example, Kokuryo and Platform Design Lab (2011) (see, Footnote 2) describes the concept of management to create emergent value by designing a communication base that promotes collaboration through the sharing of processes and interfaces for activities among organisations. This chapter examines the design of a place where employees can work while supplementing the corresponding motivation aspects of employees.

reflected in the activities. In the case of Mitsubishi Heavy Industries Group, which is somewhat exceptional, they operate the projects completely based on volunteer activities identified by employees.

Depending on how the organisation designs and communicates the social issues, the role of participating members in the project as a link between the organisation and its stakeholders will also differ. In addition, the difference in the level of abstraction when defining the social issues is also linked to the perception and cooperation of other members of the company. In that sense, the roles of participants affect exploration and exploitation.

In Yahoo Japan, some activities have been implemented and developed in relation with other associated departments and the management of the project was handed over from Ishinomaki Base to Tokyo Head Office. Thus, through the succession of activities, the influence of the results of exploration spread throughout the company. OMRON and Bridgestone authorise individual project initiated by certain department or company from the whole group through the global award system. Marui Group supports activities conducted by members of the 'official group project team' with the involvement of senior managers. Mitsubishi Heavy Industries Group fully respect and appreciate employees' willingness and spontaneity, with the aim of improving employee satisfaction through their voluntary initiatives.

It is difficult to draw any conclusions about how to indicate the direction of the activity and the extent to which participants get involved based only on the cases of the five companies. However, in comparison, the clearer the direction of the activity and the greater the degree of freedom of the participants is, the broader the range of connections can be created between internal and external stakeholders. As shown in Iris Marion Young's model of social responsibility (see Chap. 3), responsibility is socially connected with various internal and external stakeholders. Fulfilling infinite responsibility for society is an emergent process that engages various stakeholders inside or outside a company. The participants should play important roles here and value can be created with responsibility fulfilled. An organisational design supporting such a chain of connections is desirable.

9.4.2 Sharing Social Issues

To carry out emergent responsible management, a mechanism is needed to form a common understanding of social issues. In traditional management with a top-down approach, the content and goals of activity have been set at company level in advance and the workplaces must follow these instructions and policies. For example, in the case of eco-products, manufacturers will set their own eco-product certification standards and define target levels for their activities, thereby clarifying what kind of activities are and how they should be implemented. However, emergent responsible management requires a different approach. In emergent responsible management, employees who play a leading role in the implementation of activities will decide the activity content by themselves. Therefore, it is necessary to form a common understanding of social issues within the company to ensure cohesion and consistency.

As observed in OMRON and Bridgestone, the award system promotes company-wide sharing of activities through the processes including implementation of activities, application for the award, evaluation and awarding, as well as by sharing of desirable activities between employees and the management. In Bridgestone's case, the award system is a process in which the management and employees share an understanding of what activities reflect the corporate philosophy. Bridgestone's corporate philosophy of 'Serving Society with Superior Quality' can be interpreted in various ways due to its high level of abstraction and universality regardless of times and environment. The management serve as committee members and select the projects qualified for the awards to be shared with the entire group so that employees can understand what kind of activities embody the management philosophy in the current context.

The participants of the project do not specialise in undertaking social issues; thus, it is also important to seek support from experts and stakeholders who are directly involved in such social issues. In the 'official group project team' of Marui Group, industrial physicians and external lecturers are invited to provide information at monthly meetings, and members who participate in the project are able to share a common understanding of health management. With such information gained from the external experts, the project members, who are well aware of the internal situation, implement the activities by defining the related issues and working on them through trial and error. The results will be shared and discussed frequently among the members. This allows the participants in the project to refer to each other's experience and gain new perspectives, thus, broadening the range of exploration.

9.4.3 Motivation

Responsibility is inherently driven by internal motivation, which needs to be considered in a multifaceted way to implement the activities in an organisation smoothly. In the design of emergent responsible management, it is necessary to consider the motivations of employees. In the normal business, this can be achieved through accountability of subordinates to superiors, with a relationship of the granting of authority and the obligation to report. However, emergent responsible management aims to achieve responsibility beyond such type of accountability, and requires a different approach from routine management.

In this regard, in Marui Group Aoi's understanding of CSR as the president provides clues. In accordance with Aoi's advice, Marui Group has interpreted social contribution to society as 'what employees want to do'. In doing so, they have succeeded in bringing out the participants' enthusiasm. For example, Aoi thought that giving consideration to women and LGBT customers was something everyone wanted to do, even if the company did not say so. Therefore, they recruit members with open application and those who have a will to make social contributions will participate, and the role of the company should play is to create an environment to support the activities.

Marui Group's 'official group project team' selects participants who are particularly aware of the issues from employees that applied to join the project. Similarly, at Yahoo Japan, core members of the Ishinomaki Base have been selected because they are very active in the earthquake recovery projects. These members continued their activities even after the company-wide activities have been settled, which demonstrates that they have a very high awareness of social issues. These examples show that motivation problems can be solved by designing activities in a way that those who want to work on certain social issue can gather spontaneously.

You may think that setting KPIs is an effective way to manage employee behaviour and motivation. In fact, KPI-based management has been recommended and actively deployed in the CSR field, as well as in ordinary management areas. If the content of CSR activities is clearly determined, management with KPIs is effective. However, emergent responsible management, which requires employees to determine the activities spontaneously, does not fit into the idea of KPI very well because the objective is not defined in advance.

In other words, in emergent responsible management, since employees need to consider what should be done, the details of the activities and the corresponding results are not known in advance, and the activities are not homogenised. In the process of performing activities that create value through interaction, it is not possible to fully understand the causal relationship between activities and their results; thus, it is difficult to set evaluation criteria in advance by setting goals.

9.5 Combining Diverse Resources and Changing Organisational Boundaries

In this chapter, we have considered the design of emergent responsible management from the viewpoint of exploration and exploitation of knowledge based on organisational ambidexterity. In the cases discussed in this book, the process of exploration, in which employees proactively seek relationships with stakeholders, is managed through the award system or specific design of their own projects. In addition, we examined how we can make full use of the management resources that have been accumulated through exploitation, without being isolated in the organisation, and discussed how to balance social contribution activities and the business.

It is expected that the design of an emergent responsible management will lead to 'combining diverse resources' as indicated in the definition of emergence. In particular, it is important in emergent responsible management that new connections that have been overlooked in the conventional management framework will be created between external stakeholders and internal organisation members. For example, in OMRON's case, projects with social contribution that might be rejected under the conventional business could be pursued under the TOGA initiative. This creates a new connection with stakeholders. Similarly, Mitsubishi Heavy Industry Group has created a highly flexible connection with its stakeholders by setting out a considerably independent activity in which employees can voluntarily work outside business hours.

Changes in relationships with external stakeholders have also affected the way organisations work. Marui Group has been able to incorporate external knowledge into its organisational activities by inviting experts to the organisation through its 'official group project team'. In Yahoo Japan, by connecting with stakeholders beyond the framework of an organisation, they have succeeded in combining resources with a network among different organisations, which is different from that of the normal business.

By conducting emergent responsible management, various links are created between stakeholders and management resources, and value is created both for society and the organisation. The design of the organisation for this purpose not only promotes activities but also changes the boundaries of the organisation. As we have repeatedly discussed in this book, responsibility is to be fulfilled by each and every person, and the scope cannot be specified in advance. Moreover, the fulfilment of certain responsibility leads to other responsibility, which is connected one after another. If employees carry out such activities, the boundaries of the organisation will change than expected.

The transformation of corporate management is indispensable, but it is difficult to implement if it is contrary to existing methods. In emergent responsible management, companies can pursue infinite responsibility under a different dimension from ordinary business. This changes the boundaries of the organisation and leads to management transformation.

Chapter 10
The Process of Emergent Responsible Management

Mitsunobu Ando, Hirotsugu Kitada, and Katsuhiko Kokubu

Abstract The purpose of this chapter is to provide a potentially applicable process to adopt emergent responsible management. It firstly outlines the difference between the process of emergent and conventional management. After that, a five-step framework regarding how to implement emergent responsible management is illustrated and discussed in details. The concept of the responsibility to pursue is different from that in the general business; thus, it is not desirable to apply the same conventional management process. However, the operational process is often required as long as it is performed as an organisational activity. According to different situations, the proposals in this book might not always be the perfect to follow. However, in the case of emergent responsible management as a project that is performed in parallel with the general business, the effectiveness of the operation process described in this chapter can be inferred from the practices of the case companies in this book.

10.1 Differences Between Emergent and Conventional Management

Emergent responsible management is designed to make it easy for employees to fulfil infinite responsibility. In Chap. 9, we discussed how companies recognise these activities, allocate resources, and even motivate employees towards their achievement. However, such practical activities cannot be performed by design alone, and a process to manage the operations is required. It is not impossible to carry out emergent responsible management as an activity that is completely based on employees' free will. However, if the activities of emergent responsible management are performed in parallel with the strictly managed general business, it would have to compromise with the general management process.

Emergent responsible management requires a grand design that is not bound by conventional business practices, which can be achieved by formulating it as a strategy. However, it would be difficult for practitioners at the frontline to implement it in an emergent way with the strategic framework alone. Therefore, a management process

K. Kokubu et al., *Emergent Responsible Management*, Kobe University Monograph Series in Social Science Research, https://doi.org/10.1007/978-981-19-0416-5_10

supporting the introduction of emergent responsible management into business practices is necessary. However, to 'control' emergent responsible management is basically paradoxical, which may easily hinder the emergence of practice. Therefore, a new operation process for emergent responsible management is required.

To begin with, differences between the conventional and emergent management process can be mainly summarised as shown in Table 10.1. Conventional management process is applied to the general operations of many companies. A typical example is the management control process including KPIs and PDCA cycle. This type of control is also recommended in CSR activities. By contrast, emergent responsible management is based on the activities of active and spontaneous employees. Table 10.1 is based on the findings from the five case companies discussed in this book. With no doubt, this should be understood as merely a broad outline of the differences and does not include everything.

Emergent responsible management is 'management that encourages employees to take the initiative based on the concept of infinite responsibility' and can be carried out as a general business activity, as well as an independent project. The case studies in this book are either independent projects or at least, initiatives that include such activities. If the overall management of a company is conducted under infinite responsibility, the company would be similar to a teal organisation, as mentioned in Chap. 2. This may be practical in a small organisation; however, in the case of a large company, it will be difficult to make such an organisational change suddenly, and the question remains whether it is necessary. If so, as in the five case companies, implementing emergent responsible management on a project basis can be one solution. Even in project-based initiatives, these cases show that this model can contribute to promoting the integration of social issues with the general business. In this chapter, we will consider the operation process under such emergent responsible management.

Table 10.1 Differences between conventional and emergent management processes

Task	Conventional management process	Emergent management process
Job manager	Superiors	**Employees and stakeholders**
Job descriptions	Decided by superiors	**Decided by employees**
Goal setting	Decide by the company	**Decided by employees**
Nature of the goals	Mostly quantitative	**Mostly qualitative**
Attitude towards other companies in the same industry	Competitors	**Partners for solving problems**
Way of thinking regarding goals	Quota achievement	**Guidelines for problem-solving**
Performance evaluation	CSR department	**Employees**
Position of CSR department	Practitioner	**General producer**

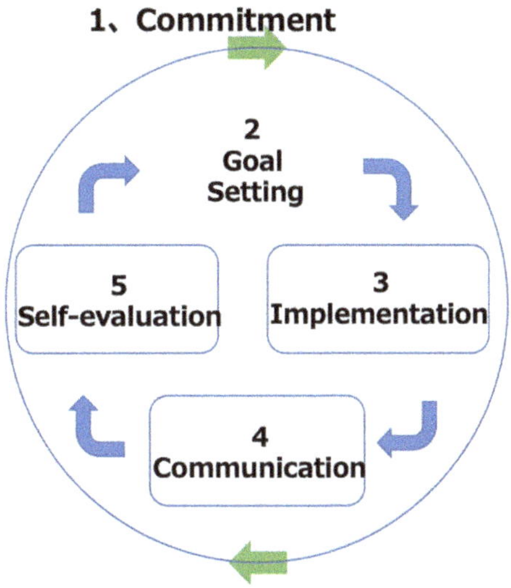

Fig. 10.1 Operation process of emergent responsible management

We are not denying conventional CSR activities that follow the general PDCA process. There are many social issues, such as environmental protection and human rights issues that need to be clearly defined and addressed. However, this alone cannot help fulfil infinite responsibility to society. There is also a way of fulfilling responsibility by getting involved in society to explore our own responsibility and implement such responsibility through trial and error. This book simply labels this type of activities as emergent responsible management and does not insist that all CSR activities should be carried out in an emergent way. Rather, we expect a synergistic effect[1]; thus, it is necessary to explicitly propose a framework for the operations of emergent responsible management.

10.2 Operations of Emergent Responsible Management

It would not be easy to spread the understanding of emergent responsible management and put it into practice if it is too far away from the general business. It should be structured in a way that inspires employees to work 'emergently' through connecting with others, while maintaining the framework of the general operations. As such, we need an operation process to translate the concept of emergent responsible management into practice and carry out the activities smoothly. As shown in Fig. 10.1, we propose a framework of the operation process, with reference to the preceding five case studies.

In Fig. 10.1, the operation is divided into five steps. The first and most important step is the *commitment* of top management and employees. In a corporate

[1] The effects of emergent responsible management are discussed in Chap. 12.

organisation, no activity can be carried out without the top management's commitment. However, in emergent responsible management, this is not enough. Responsibility is borne by each person; thus, it is necessary for employees to be aware of their commitment by themselves.

The second and third steps are *goal setting* and *implementation* by the employees, who play the leading role in these activities. The point here is that the employees should decide their goals and roles independently. It is necessary to emphasise that the company should never impose any goals or expectations. The fourth step is *communication*, whereby conversations and engagement with internal and external stakeholders are carried out according to the progress of activities. If employees or activities are isolated, social issues cannot be solved; neither can they gain empathy and trust from any stakeholders. Employees must actively communicate and engage with internal and external stakeholders.

The last step is *self-evaluation*. There are various organisational activities conducted in a company, which are basically evaluated by superiors. However, emergent responsible management is not implemented for the superior, but for society. Therefore, it is the society that should evaluate the activities. However, it is practically impossible to be evaluated by society directly, thus it should be substituted with '*self-evaluation*'. Then, by giving feedback on the results to the society and organisation, the circulation of operation in emergent responsible management is enabled.

At first glance, the process of emergent responsible management proposed here seems similar to the PDCA cycle, as in regular management process, but the practical content is actually quite different. We will specify each step in the following section.

10.3 Commitment from Top Management and Employees (Step 1)

First, it is necessary to introduce and share the concept of emergent responsible management throughout the organisation. Since emergent responsible management is an initiative that creates connections with society, which is different from the general business, it is necessary to make it clear to the whole organisation what to start with. In this process, it is important for the top management to clarify their commitment to the initiatives. This means that the top management should be aware of their responsibility and promise to pursue such responsibility through organisational activities, which has been conveyed in many corporate philosophies, as in the cases discussed previously. The corporate philosophy is manifested as the commitment of the founders or former top management over time and it is important to share that spirit.

In addition, if the top management declares putting the corporate philosophy into practice as the purpose of emergent responsible management, it is necessary for them to adopt the corporate philosophy in actual management decisions and convey it to employees. Employees can fully understand the exact role of the corporate philosophy if the top management is making decisions based on not only the economic aspects but also the corporate philosophy in the day-to-day business. This seems to be a simple task, but it is actually quite difficult. The top management is responsible for the financial performance of a company for a certain period, but emergent responsible management has no time limit. However, this management model can be realised only if this contradiction is overcome. By fully understanding such difficulty, the previous top management elaborated on the corporate philosophy to carry forward their sprit over time.

However, since the employees have to play the leading role in emergent responsible management, it is important for them to be aware of their own responsibility, which is their commitment to society. Regarding this, during the survey of the five case companies, we could clearly recognise their awareness of commitment to society when the employees we met were vividly talking about their responsibility to society. It is not necessary for employees to declare as a pledge; yet, sharing their thoughts with other project participants will be a great encouragement. It should be understood by everyone involved in emergent responsible management that the commitment of employees is as important as the commitment of the top management.

In addition, sharing the concept within the company in the initial phase is not only important for those who are directly involved in activities. To achieve substantial results from a project of emergent responsible management, it is necessary to gain understanding from superiors and other colleagues as well. Emergent responsible management respects the subjectivity of employees and thus, it is important to emphasise the independence of employees from existing business activities. Based on a trusting relationship with their employees, organisations should ensure temporal and spatial independence of the project from the existing business. Moreover, a company must also foster an organisational culture that values the personality of employees and facilitates voluntary activities.

However, a single initial declaration would not be sufficient. OMRON has succeeded in significantly increasing the number of applications after several years of TOGA. Bridgestone is also planning to spend several years disseminating its concept of *Our Way to Serve* throughout its organisation. Sufficient time is needed to incorporate this concept into the organisational culture.

10.4 Goal Setting: Flexible Goals and Planning (Step 2)

Once commitment from the top management has been made and the whole organisation begins to share a common direction, the next action is to set the goals. The necessity of the action plan depends on the practice, but goals are indispensable as the cornerstone of any activity. However, the goals of emergent responsible management must be flexible, unlike those of the general business. Society is constantly changing, and even if certain KPIs were set, they might become shortly out-of-date without leading to any results. Imperfect numerical targets can distort employees' behaviour and keep them from achieving results, leaving only negative results for the organisation in the long run. Therefore, in individual practice, it is important to set flexible indicators under a broad policy such as the corporate philosophy.

Unlike general management activities, it is not always important to achieve results in one year in emergent responsible management projects. Rather, its value is often enhanced as activities continue, such as Yahoo Japan's Fisherman Japan project and Bridgestone's support for Australia's Leukaemia Foundation. However, if no direction or goals for those activities are given to some extent, the employees might slack off on efforts in contributing to society especially during busy seasons. In fact, it would be occasionally effective to make a certain plan to manage the progress as an organisational activity.

In principle, it is desirable to make a flexible plan as well. First, it is necessary to exchange opinions with a variety of people when making a plan. In emergent responsible management, the individual employee plays the key role, but the goal is achieved through interaction with other people. In addition, there are various ways of exchanging opinions. In Bridgestone's case, the direction of the approach is decided by talking directly with stakeholders and listening to their voice. In the case of the Marui Group, the needs of external stakeholders are indirectly incorporated through the advices of experts, and such ideas gradually permeate at individual level through discussions of participants in 'the official group project teams'.

Emergent responsible management initiatives require flexibility in goals and plans because they are often carried out in a highly uncertain environment to take on unusual challenges and need cooperation with external stakeholders. Those projects try to tackle problems that so far have not been addressed by organisations. In that sense, it would be effective to leave some room to challenge freely within the organisation, such as the '15% culture'[2] in 3M, which are also adopted by other companies for innovation management.

Solving social issues must be the first priority in the goals of emergent responsible management. Social issues reflect stakeholders' needs, and the significance there existing in enterprises is to address such issues. In other words, in emergent responsible management, basically any goal can be set as long as each employee can take on social issues under the commitment made in step 1. To meet the needs of society and stakeholders, there is no point if those who are in the frontline are not involved in setting the goals and making plans. Instead, it is meaningful if an organisation can accept the goals and plans set originally by the practitioners as well as the diverse means developed by them. Since most activities cannot be performed by only an individual employee, people involved in the activities can achieve unprecedented results by crossing the boundary of general business activities, sharing goals within or beyond their departments and creating projects to make full use of individual abilities. The flexibility of goals is significant in the context of such internal collaboration.

---

[2] At 3M, there is a culture that allows 15% of working hours to be spent on research according to personal preference (from 3M's website).

The role of employees in emergent responsible management is not to fulfil the task given by their superior, but to achieve the goals determined by themselves and pursue the organisational mission through these activities. Their leader should be the employees themselves, not their superiors. It is important for employees to be aware of their own responsibility, and the operational process needs to be designed to support this. Enabling employees to feel free to challenge social issues that would have been far from the general business operations or traditional CSR activities, is one way to encourage stakeholder engagement between organisations and society.

10.5 Implementation: Establishment of an Organisational Cooperation System (Step 3)

After the direction is clarified in steps 1 and 2, the implementation begins in step 3. In emergent responsible management, although the projects are conducted by individual employees, if the activities are isolated from the organisation, the value created will also be limited. Therefore, it is desirable if the superiors of the project participants could not only understand the activities, but also take a step forward to communicate interactively with them. This could generate an emergent relation. Creating such an environment requires commitment from the top management.

Implementing emergent responsible management often requires collaboration with existing organisations, thus it would be effective for the organisation to keep track of the progress of activities and understand necessary support. Whether the members of an emergent responsible management project can play an independent role greatly depends on how their superiors understand and approach the project. In addition, superiors can be expected to help build relationships with external stakeholders in some cases. If external stakeholders, such as NGOs or government agencies, also have a similar organisational hierarchy or social status, communication may be smoothly developed with the participation of managers as a counterpart. In the case of Bridgestone, it is obvious that the intervention of the superior contributes to the development of activities. It is also effective to carry out an educational program to deepen the understanding of management at the same time. For example, the Marui Group's resilience program of the wellness program for senior managers promotes their understanding of the activities of the 'official group project team'.

Regarding the leaders of the whole activity, while most of the conventional CSR activities are led by the CSR department, from the cases introduced in this book, the CSR department is not always the main player; rather, the project members from various departments often takes the lead instead. It is desirable if the head of the project team is from senior or top management. If it is a department manager that takes the lead, the responsibility is often limited to the department in charge; thus, it is not possible to perform the activity from a bird's-eye view, thereby limiting company-wide efforts. Moreover, emergent responsible management usually has a strong sense of permeating the corporate philosophy; therefore, top management should be responsible for its promotion. The members of the leaders are definitely as important as the mechanism because they are the supporters of the emergent and spontaneous activities of the employees.

Even if a system for employees to fulfil their responsibility to society is established in steps 1 and 2, there is a great practical concern that the action of individual employee can be limited. Therefore, an organisational structure to support it is necessary. Here are two points to note in implementing the project.

The first point is to define '*success*'. What kinds of activities are considered 'successful' as emergent responsible management? The conditions for its success are not necessarily quantitatively defined. The purpose of general business activities is ultimately tied to economic outcomes and evaluated accordingly, which is different in emergent responsible management. Therefore, if the conditions and expectations for success cannot be clearly defined, employees may feel that they are forced to perform activities. Since emergent responsible management activities cannot be implemented without the cooperation of many employees, effective results will not be possible if the participants have different understanding and recognition of success. The conditions for this success must be determined by the employees themselves, but coordination among participants, as well as a mechanism to support them, are required. In addition, the creation and sharing of support tools for this purpose is also important in its promotion across the organisation.

Second, in promoting the project, it should be noted that there is no need to launch all projects as new ones. New projects need resources accordingly and are likely to be rejected by those who are bound by the existing framework, not hoping for new changes. To relieve such concerns, one possible solution is to reorganise existing activities for emergent responsible management projects. For example, Bridgestone renewed the existing corporate award system by emphasising the social roles of the company. No matter how wonderfully a project is planned, it is meaningless if it is not implemented. At the initial stage, it is also important to reduce resistance to achieve internal consensus for implementation.

10.6 Communication: Activate Internal and External Interactions (Step 4)

Communication is important in the practice of emergent responsible management. Here, communication does not merely mean the exchange of information, but also requires the involvement of other employees and external stakeholders as part of stakeholder engagement. Emergent responsible management projects are not limited to specific departments; rather, it often works as a cross-functional project. As such, internal and external communications that are always different from those of the usual operations.

For example, OMRON's TOGA encourages projects conducted by all kinds of teams with members either within certain department or from different departments.

Certainly, it is not enough to use the same communication channels as in the general business activities. In TOGA, the top management highly evaluates the 'realising corporate philosophy' project and praises the employees who made efforts for it. A virtuous cycle is thereby created where employees continue to exert effort with the encouragement of top management. Such a dialogue between the top management and employees is indispensable to emergent responsible management. Both vertical communication within the company and horizontal communication across departments are important.

Furthermore, concerning communication with top management, acquiring approval and authorisation internally are also important. The award systems adopted by OMRON and Bridgestone are typical examples. With appreciation from the top management, the motivation of employees participating in the activity is enhanced, and other employees can understand what is required from such best practices. Similarly, in the case of Yahoo Japan and Marui Group, receiving approval from the top management makes it easier to obtain cooperation from other members of the company.

In emergent responsible management, employees work on their own initiative. Even if a system is created for the entire organisation, if the activities and results of the employees are not well presented, the project may not be perfectly incorporated into the organisation. When conducting emergent responsible management as a project, there is a risk that it may result in partial optimisation due to the promotion of individual projects, leading to a lack of the synergistic effects. Therefore, it is necessary to communicate in various ways and promote internal conversations. For example, it is effective to make full use of intranet and in-house newsletter. Regardless of what method they use, enhance the visibility of activities and outcomes may facilitate communication. As a result, the internal communication is initiated with such engagement and will be promoted throughout the company at an accelerated rate. Therefore, if the CSR department is involved in emergent responsible management, it may be desirable for it to take on a coordinating role that supports and organises the activities rather than being the main player.

For example, the Kizuna Activities in Mitsubishi Heavy Industries Group, where employees get together outside the normal working hour to engage in activities that contribute to society, works as a project to support employees' spontaneous activities and helps in promoting communication. Although it is an activity after work, the company provides a mechanism that allows employees to independently launch projects and participate in activities of their own interest. This scheme promotes communication between participants and external stakeholders, thereby breaking down the barriers.

Recently, since the evaluation of employees in an organisation is becoming more and more result-oriented, the performance of individuals is emphasised, and interaction with employees outside the organisation considerably decreases. As a result, it is even difficult to build cooperative and trust relationship among internal members, thus there is a danger that communication in an organisation is greatly impaired. However, emergent responsible management is not conducted for profit, neither is it evaluated based on performance; rather, it provides a mechanism to break down such internal barriers and increase employees' motivation for improving society as well as the company. In this way, there is great possibility to promote internal communication by promoting emergent responsible management.

It is the same in external communication. To fulfil our responsibility to society is to join the social connections of responsibility. Therefore, practising emergent responsible management helps organisations to open up to society as a new communication circuit, which is evident in all five cases. As pointed out at the end of Chap. 9, emergent responsible management is about changing the boundaries of an organisation by shaping the relationship between the organisation and society, and value is created along with this change.

Therefore, it is necessary to systematically keep up external communications as an organisation. Even if relationships have been established in individual projects, it often disappears over time, which is a pity. While there is no need to maintain unnecessary relationships, good communication networks with society could further strengthen the social foundation of the organisation.

10.7 Self-evaluation: Feedback to Oneself and the Organisation (Step 5)

Emergent responsible management aims to take on responsibility to society as an individual working in an organisation; thus, it is the society that should make the assessment if evaluation is needed. However, this is generally difficult; therefore, we need self-evaluation instead, which means reflection on activities to fulfil the responsibility. If employees report such reflection regularly, they can provide details of the activities and receive feedback from the organisation, so that the process of emergent responsible management is continued in a virtuous cycle. Moreover, although it is self-evaluation, by working on the evaluation process, there is a merit that the shape of the process can stay consistent with that of the general management process.

One of the important points of self-evaluation is to make practitioner's personal experience seen and known, which can make the results clearer and provide feedback to the project team. Both quantitative and qualitative assessment can be used to present the results. Awards from organisations, such as in the cases of OMRON and Bridgestone, are also one kind of important feedbacks given by the organisation. If communication is actively promoted based on such signalling, employees can objectively view their own activities to some extent and improve the activity. In this case, even without KPIs, activities should be naturally improved and carried out.

For example, SOMPO Holdings (hereinafter, SOMPO), of which the operations are not introduced in this book as an individual case, but was also interviewed during the survey, conducts very unique CSR management. SOMPO uses a CSR implementation plan as an action management tool for CSR initiatives. By applying this management tool in each branch, CSR has been incorporated into the organisation's action plan and the general work of each employee. The unique point of the SOMPO case is that employees plan, implement, evaluate, and improve their activities by themselves. In conventional CSR activities, the management or CSR department would decide the content of the activity, and then give instructions to the employees in the frontline to carry it out. However, SOMPO undertook a different way of management by enhancing their support for employees who practise the PDCA cycle by themselves. In addition, a CSR supporter called 'CSR checker' is assigned to all workplaces, and more than 2,800 'CSR checkers' work actively throughout the company.[3] This is an example of self-evaluation and feedback in which employees are required to take charge of the management of CSR initiatives, from setting goals by themselves to measuring the effects.

In a traditional management process, it is the superiors that decide what the subordinates should do and how to evaluate it. However, in emergent responsible management, it is fundamental that employees should not only carry out the activities but also evaluate the results; thus, they also have to verify whether the self-evaluation is reasonable. To this end, it is better to utilise various means of feedback. It is effective to hold a meeting in the company for individual activities and receive evaluations from colleagues. If possible, it is also fruitful to invite external stakeholders to evaluate the results of the activities. This is not only a means of providing information to the society, but also of receiving feedback from the society, which makes stakeholder engagement more active.

However, we have to note that there is a risk that the feedback process can easily turn into a formality through repetition, which is the same in self-evaluation if applied in the form of scores. In this regard, it is necessary to keep constantly seeking for improvement with the understanding that emergent responsible management is an act of fulfilling responsibility. Responsibility can never be fulfilled '*completely*' because responsibility is infinite. Therefore, it is necessary to receive feedback for self-evaluation, which will benefit the next activity. If you fulfil certain responsibility, there comes the next one immediately. Making effective use of this cycle is the key to the emergent responsible management process.

10.8 Making the Most of Emergent Responsible Management

In this chapter, we have proposed a five-step framework regarding how to implement emergent responsible management. The concept of the responsibility to pursue is different from that in the general business; thus, it is not desirable to apply the same conventional management process. However, the operational process is often required as long as it is performed as an organisational activity. That is why we address this issue in this chapter.

---

[3] From SOMPO Holdings' *CSR Communication Report 2018.*

Obviously, depending on the type of emergent responsible management, such a process may not be necessary, or an entirely new type of process might be effective. In that sense, the proposals in this book are by no means unique. However, in the case of emergent responsible management as a project that is performed in parallel with the general business, the effectiveness of the operation process described in this chapter can be inferred from the practices of the case companies in this book.

Nevertheless, an incorrect use of goals and evaluations can undermine emergent responsible management. In addition, there is a possibility that the superior–subordinate relationship in the hierarchy of the company can either contribute to or hinder the spontaneity and independence of employees. In the implementation of emergent responsible management, it is necessary to pay close attention to this point. Especially for those who are fully accustomed to the general business activities, they may not immediately understand the idea that goals must be flexible or self-assessment is good. Only the top management can finally persuade them, and what encourages the top management to take such actions is the corporate philosophy. In emergent responsible management, even if it is a project-based activity, there is a risk of getting stuck quickly if not operated under such an overall design.

Current CSR activities have traditionally tended to focus on '*what to do*' or '*how to do it*', while the discussion of the premise of these activities, namely '*why do it*' has always been greatly overlooked. However, in companies that are devoted to realising social value creation, such as the case companies mentioned in this book, the prerequisites are the basis of operation, and these support the daily activities of employees who create value. That is why we believe that emergent responsible management is effective in challenging more essential social issues and creating greater social value.

Chapter 11
Challenging SDGs with Emergent Responsible Management

Kimitaka Nishitani and Katsuhiko Kokubu

Abstract In this chapter, we examine how emergent responsible management can be applied to new issues such as fulfilling sustainable development goals (SDGs). After briefly discussing what SDGs are and the SDGs Guideline for companies, this chapter illustrates the significance and limitations of working on the SDGs as the main business and proposes that emergent responsible management can be employed to achieve the SDGs more certainly. SDGs are currently receiving increasing attention, and emergent responsible management would be effective in reformulating these SDGs-related activities as enduring initiatives. To work on the SDGs in emergent responsible management, it is important to regard the activities on SDGs in terms of infinite responsibility and focus on the spontaneity of employees. It is also important to note that the SDGs work as a very suggestive framework in view of the relationship between infinite responsibility and finite accountability. Considering this, the SDGs can be regarded as activities that aim at infinite responsibility (goals) by continuously working on finite responsibility (targets). In this sense, the chapter suggests the potential of emergent responsible management to perpetuate the goals of the SDGs and the relationship between goals and targets can provide future direction for it.

11.1 How Can a Company Tackle the Sustainable Development Goals?

Since the United Nations adopted the Sustainable Development Goals (SDGs) in 2015, the SDGs have gained great attention in the world. Corporate sustainability reports are decorated with the SDGs logo; many symposia and seminars on this topic are held; and various SDG awards are proposed. In commercial streets, it is not uncommon to find people with 17-colour SDGs lapel pins. However, it remains questionable as to whether companies are really working on the SDGs.

The SDGs are basically goals that are achieved through governmental obligation, thus although efforts from private companies are acknowledged, this is not a legal

The original version of this chapter was revised: Belated corrections received in Chapters 1, 2, 9 and 11 have been updated. The correction to this chapter is available at https://doi.org/10.1007/978-981-19-0416-5_13

K. Kokubu et al., *Emergent Responsible Management*, Kobe University Monograph Series in Social Science Research, https://doi.org/10.1007/978-981-19-0416-5_11

duty. However, if companies emphasise their SDGs activities in their reports without any substance, this may be criticised as 'SDGs washing'. More importantly, if the SDGs are goals to be fulfilled by the whole world by 2030, everyone shares those responsibilities as an individual. Therefore, any activity that seeks private benefit under the name of the SDGs must be admonished.

In this sense, the common slogan of pursuing the SDGs to achieve economic and social benefit simultaneously should be reconsidered from the perspective of emergent responsible management. Obviously, if the SDGs are pursued to achieve social benefits, and an economic benefit is also achieved *as a result*, there is no problem. However, if SDG-related activities are carried out for economic benefits, it is the same as a normal business, and this is absolutely 'SDGs washing'.

Therefore, we believe that if a company works on the SDGs, it should be performed as part of activities concerning infinite responsibility. However, it is often claimed that to undertake the SDGs is a business opportunity or a means to enhance corporate reputation. To warn against such trends and return to the original spirit of the SDGs, this chapter examines the way companies challenge the SDGs from the perspective of emergent responsible management.

11.2 What Are the SDGs?

The SDGs were set as an international agenda to create a sustainable society through 17 goals (1. no poverty, 2. zero hunger, 3. good health and well-being, 4. quality education, 5. gender equality, 6. clean water and sanitation, 7. affordable and clean energy, 8. decent work and economic growth, 9. industry innovation and infrastructure, 10. reduced inequalities, 11. sustainable cities and communities, 12. responsible consumption and production, 13. climate action, 14. life below water, 15. life on land, 16. peace, justice, and strong institutions, and 17. partnership for the goals) and their accompanying 169 targets, as described in the 'Transforming Our World: The 2030 Agenda for Sustainable Development', which was unanimously adopted by the 193 member countries at the United Nations Summit in September 2015. Figure 11.1 shows the logo of the 17 SDGs. Building on the success of 'Millennium Development Goals' (MDGs) from 2001 to 2015, SDGs set out the priorities for sustainable development and what the world should do for it from 2016 to 2030. While the MDGs were more about goals for developing countries, the SDGs are universal goals that need to be worked at by all countries, whether developing or developed.

Based on the inclusive pledge of 'no one left behind', these goals encompass a wide range of issues to achieve a sustainable society including those that were not achieved by the MDGs, those that were not included in the MDGs, and those that have newly emerged. Since these issues to be resolved in the SDGs arose from various socio-economic activities, they reflect the economic, social, and environmental aspects in a cross-sectional way. Thus, all stakeholders are expected to play their respective roles to achieve the SDGs and to comprehensively work in three areas: economic, social, and environmental. In addition, transparency and accountability are important to ensure that everyone is involved in the activities.

Fig. 11.1. 17 Sustainable Development Goals. *Source* Website of United Nations Information Centre

Although the SDGs are not legally binding, monitoring indicators and regular follow-up are necessary, which requires governments to not only promote regional policies but also follow up and verify the progress accordingly. In Japan, in May 2016, the 'SDGs Promotion Headquarters' was established in the Cabinet with all ministers as members. In December of the same year, the *SDGs Implementation Guideline* that matched the SDGs in the Japanese context was issued. In addition, the SDGs Promotion Roundtable was set up under the SDGs Promotion Headquarters, where stakeholders exchange opinions to facilitate cooperation. Meanwhile, to encourage companies and organisations to work on activities to achieve the SDGs, the Japan SDGs Award, which commends companies and organisations that have made excellent efforts to achieve the SDGs, has been established. Winners are selected based on the opinions of the selection committee consisting of members of the SDGs Promotion Roundtable.

11.3 SDG Guidelines for Companies

The SDGs position private organisation as one of the prime actors, and require their cooperation in solving issues for sustainable development in a creative and innovative way. In addition, many responsible investment funds, which invest in companies considering environment, society, and governance issues, are also supportive of the SDGs. For example, in Japan, the Government Pension Investment Fund (GPIF) takes SDG-related initiatives of companies into consideration when making their investment decisions. Thus, there is growing interest in companies that work on the SDGs. Reflecting these trends, Global Reporting Initiative (GRI), the United Nations Global Compact (UNGC) and the World Business Council for Sustainable Development (WBCSD) collaboratively published *SDG Compass*[1] as action guidelines on how companies should actually respond to the SDGs. This is a helpful guideline for companies to work on the SDGs.

The purpose of the *SDG Compass* is to provide guidance to companies on how to align their business strategies to the SDGs, measure their contributions, and manage the implementation. The process of introducing SDGs into companies is divided into five steps as below:

Step 1 Understanding the SDGs
Step 2 Defining priorities
Step 3 Setting goals
Step 4 Integrating
Step 5 Reporting and communicating.

The *SDG Compass* recommends that companies work on the SDGs as the main business by specifying materiality, setting KPIs, and implementing the PDCA cycle. This document describes the economic benefit that can be an incentive for companies to work on SDGs as follows.

> Covering a wide spectrum of sustainable development topics relevant to companies, such as poverty, health, education, climate change and environmental degradation, the SDGs can help to connect business strategies with global priorities. Companies can use the SDGs as an overarching framework to shape, steer, communicate and report their strategies, goals and activities, allowing them to capitalize on a range of benefits such as: 'identifying future business opportunities', 'enhancing value of corporate sustainability', 'strengthening stakeholder relations and keeping the pace with policy developments', 'stabilizing societies and markets', and 'using a common language and shared purpose.[2]

Furthermore, the SDG Compass proposes specific approaches that can strike a balance between society and the economy—'value-chain mapping' and 'outside-in' approaches—and these have already attracted attention in business practice. The value-chain mapping approach refers to the method of assessing the current and future positive and negative social and environmental impacts throughout the company's entire value chain from the supply base and inbound logistics, across production and operations, to the distribution, use and end-of-life of products, and to define priorities where the greatest effect on the SDGs can be expected. Meanwhile, the outside-in approach refers to the method for companies to bridge the gap between current performance and required performance by looking at what is needed externally from a global perspective and setting goals accordingly.

---

[1] https://sdgcompass.org.

[2] This explanation is a partial summary of the 'Overview' section of the *SDG Compass*.

It is understood that the outside-in approach can be used to induce innovation, reduce potential risks, and provide new business opportunities. In this way, the *SDG Compass* recommends working on SDGs as the main business that can simultaneously pursue economic benefit because the expected contribution of corporate activities to the SDGs is very great, aiming to attract as many companies as possible.

Such a link between the SDGs and the economic benefit of companies can be also seen in other SDGs guidelines. For example, the *SDG Industry Matrix* published by KPMG and the UNGC provides ideas and examples that take into account industry characteristics for each of the 17 goals and encourages companies to create common values.[3] Keidanren (Japan Business Foundation) has revised the 'Charter of Corporate Behaviour' in which the achievement of the SDGs through the realisation of Society 5.0[4] is focused. This also emphasises linkages with economic benefit. In this Charter, Keidanren stated the following 'Three Business Principles for Realizing Society 5.0' in order to succeed in business towards the achievement of Society 5.0:

(1) Creating an Innovative business model,
(2) Constantly creating new knowledge through innovation to develop superior products and services, and
(3) Creating rules that reflect the perspectives of the SDGs and contribute to improving international competitiveness for creating new markets.

In compliance with these corporate action guidelines, an increasing number of companies have declared that they will actively work on the SDGs as their main business. This is because some of the goals of the SDGs can be easily linked to business strategies even for companies that emphasise economic benefit, and a win–win relationship with their main business can be expected. For this reason, there is a tendency that the SDGs are regarded as synonymous with CSV. It is very important to integrate the SDGs into the core business as long as companies work on the SDGs. However, if working on the SDGs becomes the same as working on ordinary businesses, such activities could not fulfil the originally expected responsibility to society. It seems that few companies are aware of this problem. However, we should take this seriously from now, given the 2030 deadline.

[3] https://www.unglobalcompact.org/library/3111.

[4] Society 5.0 is 'A human-centred society that balances economic advancement with the resolution of social problems by a system that highly integrates cyberspace and physical space.' It was proposed in the 5th Science and Technology Basic Plan by the Japanese government as a future society that Japan should aspire to. It follows the hunting society (Society 1.0), agricultural society (Society 2.0), industrial society (Society 3.0), and information society (Society 4.0). Please refer to the website of the Japanese government: https://www8.cao.go.jp/cstp/english/society5_0/index.html.

11.4 Significance and Limitations of Working on the SDGs as the Main Business

According to the Japanese Ministry of the Environment's 'Environmentally Friendly Corporate Behaviour Survey' (FY2016), the main answer to the question 'Which of the following best describes the position of environmental conservation activities in your company?' is 'One of the most important social responsibilities' (74.4%), and this has a big lead over other answers such as 'One of the important strategies' (6.6%), and 'Business opportunity' (5.6%).[5] However, as CSR has become a continual practice of companies, the creation of value through CSR has gained great attention and the concept of CSV has emerged. Nonetheless, as discussed in Chap. 1, it is not easy to separate CSR, CSV, and the main business, and companies cannot handle CSV very well. This holds true when trying to pursue the SDGs as the main business.

In fact, under circumstances where the economic aspects are taken into account in solving social issues, if economic values take precedence over social values, even the most urgent social issues can be neglected. This is especially true if the SDGs are viewed as a means of economic activity, and it would be difficult to refute if such activities are criticised for pursuing economic value regardless of the SDGs. Clearly, we also need to take these important facts into considerations when working on the SDGs using the value-chain mapping and outside-in approaches.

The value-chain mapping approach links the SDGs to the value chain to identify priorities for companies to work on. However, as long as the economic value is prioritised, companies may not work on any unprofitable activities, even if it is identified by the value-chain mapping. Thus, the value-chain mapping approach may end up just identifying the priorities without any further activities in some cases. Moreover, if a company links its existing activities to the SDGs, it will be nothing more than the aforementioned 'SDGs washing'.

By contrast, it is expected that active efforts to solve social issues using the outside-in approach will lead to innovation, but innovation cannot be so easily realised. In fact, although the idea of inducing innovation by leveraging the solution of social issues, such as the 'Porter Hypothesis',[6] which advocates the positive relationship between environmental regulation and competitive advantage, has existed for a long time, there is still controversy over whether such an idea is truly effective. Therefore, as long as the economic aspects are taken into account, once innovation does not occur as expected, activities for solving social issues may likely fail eventually.

[5] The numbers are totals for listed and unlisted companies.

[6] 'Porter's hypothesis' is a concept formulated by Professor Michel Porter at Harvard Business School stating that appropriate environmental regulations trigger corporate innovation, which gives them a competitive advantage (for companies in countries without such regulations).

The problem that the role of solving social issues (as originally entrusted) cannot be sufficiently fulfilled because of overemphasising economic benefits when working on the SDGs as the main business can be conceptualised as shown in Fig. 11.2. This figure shows that the balance of society and the economy, that is often emphasised as the strength of fulfilling social responsibilities as the main business, namely position ②, is not actually the only equilibrium point for a company. In other words, if economic aspects take precedence over social aspects, position ④, which prioritises the economy at the expense of society, can also be an equilibrium point. However, it is clear that position ①, which is desirable for society but sacrifices the economy, is unlikely to be an equilibrium point unless companies have financial strength.

In other words, the 'win' of society does not always guarantee the 'win' of the business and vice versa, although conducting SDG initiatives as the main business looks very attractive because social value creation may develop business opportunity for companies. Even if the shift of the equilibrium point from position ① to ② is aimed for through an *outside-in* approach, since that approach will not necessarily lead to economic outcomes, there is a high possibility of staying in ① unless any innovation happens, without which the activity will not continue.

However, when companies work on the SDGs, if the economic outcome is zero or negative, it will be the same as charity activities. In this case, we cannot continuously demand companies to work on the SDGs. To carry out the SDGs through the main business and to fulfil responsibility, a different method from the ordinary business is required, but discussion on this point is lacking.

The idea that linking the SDGs to the main business to solve social issues can also have a positive effect on the business sounds very attractive and can be a motivation for working on the SDGs for many companies. However, the equation 'social value = economic value' may not always be achieved for all social issues as mentioned

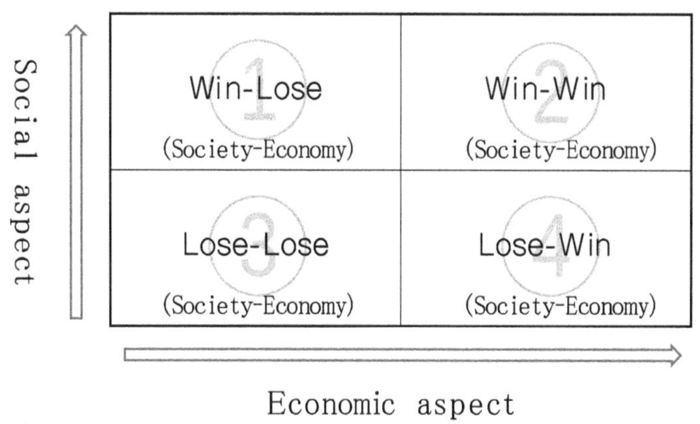

Fig. 11.2 Relationship between social and economic aspects

above, and it may just increase 'SDGs washing' unintentionally. Therefore, when working on the SDGs as the main business, it is necessary to overcome the problem that economic results are likely to be prioritised by another approach. In this respect, the concept of emergent responsible management is expected to play an important role.

11.5 Achieving the SDGs More Certainly with Emergent Responsible Management

The first thing to keep in mind when working on the SDGs in emergent responsible management is to regard the activities on SDGs in terms of infinite responsibility. Since a company is an economic organisation, it is not practical to ignore profits when working on the SDGs. However, if a company focuses on the period of commitment rather than the profit, the SDGs can be handled by approaches different from those of the usual business. In the usual business, the profitability of each project is strictly controlled, and it is necessary to withdraw from the business that does not make a profit, which is appropriate. However, if the company evaluates activities on SDGs by the rate of return as the same in the usual business, and easily withdraw them when these activities do not make a profit, this does not mean that companies have fulfilled their responsibility or that they have worked on the SDGs.

Of course, it is difficult for companies to continue low-margin projects. However, the SDGs are goals until 2030; thus, if companies promise to commit to their activities until 2030, companies can clearly differentiate SDG activities from those related to their usual business. It may be questionable that this can be called infinite responsibility, but it is certain that such activities get closer to the practices of infinite responsibility in terms of breaking the limits of normal revenue management standards.

Currently, the SDGs logo is highlighted in the sustainability reports of many companies, but there are few cases where companies regard the SDG projects as a commitment that lasts until 2030. While some companies have set ultra-long-term goals (e.g. until 2050 for decarbonisation, etc.), such goals are too far away and have little to do with specific current activities. The SDGs are highly predictable, near-future goals (until 2030). If a company declares that it will work on the SDGs, it will also need to promise to continue its activities until 2030.

Another significant aspect of working on the SDGs as emergent responsible management is to focus on the spontaneity of employees. The SDGs are a comprehensive system with 17 goals and 169 targets. It is not always easy to understand where and how SDGs are related to corporate activities. To challenge such a huge and vague area, the spontaneity of each employee is indispensable. This is the same process where employees recognise social issues. To understand how the expertise and the enormous resources of a company are related to the goals and targets of the

SDGs, the power of employees who are engaged in diversified daily tasks is essential. Without such a process, innovation through the SDGs could not be expected.

To accomplish this, first of all, each employee must understand the SDGs. In this regard, spreading information and holding seminars using in-house public relations are effective means, but activities in which employees can take the initiative to deepen their understanding of SDGs and its solutions and share such information within the company would be more effective.

For example, Sumitomo Chemical Ltd., a recipient of the Japan SDGs Award, is a company actively working on the SDGs. It has carried out a group-wide employee participation initiative, 'Our Sustainable Tree', where all employees and executive officers express their views on the SDGs by posting them on a designated website.[7] This project targets at all group employees in Japan and overseas. Each employee understands the SDGs, provides ideas about contributing to the SDGs through their usual business, volunteer activities and daily life, and then posts those ideas on a dedicated website. The main focus of this project is on letting employees think about what else they can do through work and life to achieve the SDGs. Although 'Our Sustainable Tree' project does not directly lead to solutions to SDGs issues, it can be regarded as a platform for addressing the SDGs through emergent responsible management by making employees understand the SDGs.

Emergent responsible management can be broadly classified into three types: 'corporate philosophy-driven', 'social problem-oriented', and 'spontaneity-oriented' as discussed in Chap. 9. Since employees' understanding of the SDGs itself evokes employees' spontaneity, the 'social problem-oriented' and 'spontaneity-oriented' approach can be applied relatively smoothly to the SDG activities.

For example, the photo cleaning project of Mitsubishi Heavy Industries Group's Kizuna Activities can be regarded as an activity related to SDGs Goal 11—'Sustainable cities and communities'—in terms of supporting the mental aspects of victims of the Great East Japan Earthquake. This activity was originally proposed by an employee who had been volunteering for restoration following the earthquake by herself, and the idea actually started when she understood the local situation through volunteer activities and thought that she had to do something. In the Kizuna Activities, positive effects on the main business are also expected through an increase in employee satisfaction as a result of their social contributions. That is, although emergent responsible management is not an activity directly aimed at increasing economic value, such an example suggests that employee-led activities can have a positive effect on the main business as well. It would be desirable to conduct activities that prioritise social benefits, which may eventually lead to economic effects as well. However, the prioritisation that society comes first and the economy, second, must not be reversed.

[7] Sumitomo Chemical website: https://www.sumitomo-chem.co.jp/english/sustainability/sdgs/sustainabletree.

Meanwhile, 'corporate philosophy-driven' activities are highly compatible with guidelines such as the *SDG Compass* because employees themselves will consider the social issues to be solved and link them to their main business. Therefore, as with the case of CSV, 'corporate philosophy-driven' activities are not only relatively easy for many companies to work on, but also make it easier for employees to take on the SDGs spontaneously by its certain framework. For example, OMRON's TOGA project that match the social needs of inexperienced people who seek full-time employment and SMEs who lack manpower can be regarded as an activity related with SDGs Goal 8—'Decent work and economic growth'. This project can also be evaluated as being successful for society as well as for business. As seen in other examples of 'corporate philosophy-driven' activities, supporting the activities as a company could be a great opportunity to stimulate emergent responsible management towards the SDGs.

Emergent responsible management can be expected to have a great effect on the SDGs. However, the question of whether emergent responsible management alone is enough to respond to global issues addressed in SDGs may arise. However, it does not have a specific format and can be adapted to the situation based on the concept of infinite responsibility. Any company can apply the concept of emergent responsible management when working on the SDGs. The SDGs are primarily the responsibility of the country, and cooperation from companies in the private sector is acknowledged. Thus, it is expected that companies will be able to expand their future prospects by working on emergent activities using the ingenuity of employees and emphasising various connections.

Finally, it should be pointed out that the SDGs work as a very suggestive framework in view of the relationship between infinite responsibility and finite accountability. The SDGs consist of 17 goals and 169 targets for a limited time period up to 2030. However, the 17 goals do not end in 2030, as these goals represent challenges that should be pursued forever as long as human society continues. For example, achieving no poverty (Goal 1) by a particular year is a task with finite responsibility, but maintaining it is a task of infinite responsibility.

Considering this, the SDGs can be regarded as activities that aim at infinite responsibility (goals) by continuously working on finite responsibility (targets). In this sense, emergent responsible management can be used to perpetuate the goals of the SDGs and the relationship between goals and targets can provide future direction for it.

Chapter 12
Effects of Emergent Responsible Management

Katsuhiko Kokubu

Abstract This chapter provides a comprehensive discussion on the effect of adopting emergent responsible management. Although the cases we have presented in this book are illustrated with project-based activities, emergent responsible management can theoretically be developed on a company-wide basis. As indicated by its name, emergent responsible management mainly focuses on responsibility, which implies practice. Fulfilling responsibility to others is synonymous with creating value for others, but this is not the only effect. As has been warned many times in this book, taking action with the intention of achieving certain effect is contrary to the essence of emergent responsible management, because in such a case an action is only a means, not the end. However, it is worthwhile to understand what the resulting effect is as long as this point is taken into account. Drawing on what we have discussed so far, this chapter points out some issues that have to be discussed regarding effects of practising emergent responsible management. Some insights for future development of the debate are also proposed.

12.1 Emergent Responsible Management as a Practice

In this book, 'management that encourages spontaneous activities by employees based on the concept of infinite responsibility and creates emergent practices' is called emergent responsible management. We examined some key concepts and elements underpinning the theory of emergent responsible management and investigated the cases of five companies. Consequently, some ideas were proposed for the design and process of emergent responsible management. In addition, we explored how this model can be applied to new issues such as the SDGs. While it is a normative model based on infinite responsibility, as seen from the cases in this book, we believe that it has already been implemented in practice, even though partially.

The activities of the five cases companies are not undertaken in consciousness of emergent responsible management, and it is difficult to say that infinite responsibility has been fully taken on through their practice. However, it is true that there are some activities beyond the finite 'responsibility' that is common in normal business. In this

K. Kokubu et al., *Emergent Responsible Management*, Kobe University Monograph Series in Social Science Research, https://doi.org/10.1007/978-981-19-0416-5_12

book, we have carefully discussed how we can theoretically position this concept, support it through management, and apply it to solve social issues.

However, it may seem that emergent responsible management can only be implemented as a corporate project. It is just because the examples presented in this book focus on project-based activities. Emergent responsible management can theoretically be developed on a company-wide basis, for example in teal organisations or under holacracy management. Nevertheless, the central issue in this book is not the transformation of corporate organisations, but how to solve social issues in an organisational society, especially in a large-scale organisational society. Furthermore, we have to focus on how we can restore the wholeness of a human being to enable living a satisfying life through such activities. Organisational management and its methods are just the means to this end. Therefore, we have discussed project-based initiatives that can be possibly carried out by most companies.

As indicated by its name, emergent responsible management mainly focuses on responsibility, which implies practice, rather than merely the mechanism. Therefore, the supporting mechanism needs to be constantly improved to fit the practice. The design and process of emergent responsible management described in this book is just one proposition and it should be adjusted according to the situation to achieve better results. To keep the practice functioning well, the systems and mechanisms that support it must also be designed flexibly.

Since the activity is conducted by human, it always has various effects on the surroundings. Fulfilling responsibility to others is synonymous with creating value for others, but this is not the only effect. As has been warned many times in this book, taking action with the intention of achieving certain effect is contrary to the essence of emergent responsible management, because in such a case an action is only a means, not the end. However, it is worthwhile to understand what the resulting effect is as long as this point is taken into account. We will summarise what we have discussed so far by considering the effects of practicing emergent responsible management.

12.2 Effects on Society

Emergent responsible management is based on fulfilling one's responsibility to others; thus, its effects on society should be discussed first. We are surrounded by various problems in modern society including global environment protection, economic disparity, regional depopulation, population decline in developed countries, as well as population growth issues in developing countries. Unfortunately, we cannot solve most of them by ourselves and this fact may make us pretend not to be aware of these issues. However, the problems that can be solved would substantially increase if we could use the resources of companies. Emergent responsible management encourages this by having people who can utilize and apply available resources take the responsibility.

Traditionally, it is the government that is supposed to solve social issues. However, with globalisation, what governments can do has become less, with the role of companies becoming increasingly important. This is why companies are required to be socially responsible on a global scale. However, only humans can ultimately fulfil their responsibility, and organisations can only divide or assign the given responsibility. Most of the responsibility that can be divided or assigned is finite responsibility of a limited scope. This is fundamentally different from infinite responsibility with undefined scope. Therefore, fundamental difference exists between traditional CSR activities and emergent responsible management. However, if CSR activities could be conducted under infinite responsibility, it will be emergent responsible management, as is introduced in this book.

The most important thing in practising emergent responsible management is not to fulfil the assigned responsibility, but to conduct something in the awareness of one's own responsibility. In fact, the tasks given as corporate responsibility can only be solved through individual activities, which are not specified in ISO26000 or the SDGs as well; thus, the spontaneous initiative of the actor is required. Therefore, responsibility is something that we must always seek for.

Given this perspective, emergent responsible management appears to be an engine that could automatically solves social issues. When people notice a person who is in need, they will naturally feel the desire to help. This is a subjective feeling, as well as an emotion that emerges in oneself, as inspired by others. This is the root of emergence with responsibility. The key to emergent responsible management is to try to translate it into organisational actions.

Certainly, emergent responsible management cannot be used to solve all the problems faced by society. It is also necessary to deal with the issues to be solved with a comprehensive framework such as the SDGs. However, when putting it into corporate practice, without the concept of infinite responsibility, it would quickly turn into general business, and it would be cut off eventually if the economic effect on the business is not clear. Emergent responsible management would not work out this way.

In addition, as previously pointed out, such human behaviour as pursuing infinite responsibility could also reduce the risks of society as a whole. There would be no problem if all the risks in the world could be measured and allocated to those who should be responsible. However, this is impossible because there still remain risks that cannot be recognised and measured by human beings. Faced with such risks, any risk management method is ineffective. However, if each person could deal with the world based on their infinite responsibility, it would be possible to prevent many risks in advance by adding up every small effort.

12.3 Effects on Humans

Since responsibility is to respond to the call of others, value is basically created for others. However, those who fulfil it are also affected accordingly. In particular, we can fully understand from the examples introduced in this book that the effect is not so small especially for people working in a company. Human beings, like animals or plants, are essentially complete as living creatures. However, humans in modern society live in a system where no one can survive without the help of others, which leads to a sense of suffocation shared by many people nowadays.

The larger the organisation is, the stronger this tendency is in organisational activities. An organisation includes a group of people who share the same purpose. To achieve such a purpose, the work is divided and assigned to people as 'accountability', and these people may get punished if not getting it done. Such a method is effective and efficient to achieve a specific target, but as a result, people lose their wholeness. When running a large organisation, division of work is inevitable, but the loss of wholeness needs to be addressed somehow.

As mentioned several times in this book, Laloux named the organisation that restores the wholeness of human beings as a *teal organisation* and emphasises the need to evolve into this level. Although this book does not call for organisational changes towards a teal organisation, we claim that participants can regain wholeness of work with the practice of emergent responsible management. In the cases in this book, the wholeness of work—planning, operating, and executing a project—is maintained. It is very important that participants have a sense of accomplishment that can hardly be achieved through the traditional division of labour.

It has been shown in previous studies that employees can improve their job satisfaction through CSR activities. It is also shown in the cases in this book that with the practice of emergent responsible management, the satisfaction of the participants and their commitment to the organisation have been enhanced, which has a positive effect on their ordinary work as well. In addition, it is important to note that the company should not only make evaluations with economic measures but also support the creation of social value to foster employees' trust in the organisation. Since employees are also citizens and members of society, how the organisation they work for approaches the society has a great effect on their pride and sense of security.

The discussion above points out the issues that need to be carefully considered and has a lot to do with the work style reform that has gained great attention recently in Japan. At present, a diversity of working style is required due to the diversification of social life, but it does not seem that sufficient discussion has been made on what criteria should be used for diversification of working style. If we design the working style of employees based on the concept of emergent responsible management, we believe that a new direction can be found. In other words, if a company allows employees to design their working style to fulfil the social responsibility they recognise spontaneously, it is possible that these activities will naturally work out without any particular system.

12.4 Effect on Management

Emergent responsible management will not only affect society and human beings, but also management, as is clearly indicated by the cases in this book. However, we must take care when considering these effects because emergent responsible management may easily be misunderstood as a means to achieving certain benefits for business. In fact, it must be recognised that a positive effect can only be expected *as an unexpected result* instead.

As has been warned many times in this book, if you work on emergent responsible management because it provides some benefits to the company, it would not be about fulfilment of responsibility, but turn out to be another type of profitable activity. It is the duty of human beings to fulfil their responsibility; without keeping this in mind, the practice will not be emergent responsible management. This order determines the ethic and should never be reversed. Taking this point into consideration, we will discuss the effect on management.

For management, the greatest effect of emergent responsible management is the potential to reshape the boundaries of an organisation. As organisations resemble living creatures, they need to recreate their boundaries constantly using external interfaces. Otherwise, it is difficult to survive in a highly uncertain environment. Companies should always be aware of this and spare no effort in creating new businesses. However, developing new business is not easy; rather, it requires more 'grassroots' activities, which can be addressed by emergent responsible management.

There are various types of emergent responsible management. For example, in the case of OMRON or Yahoo Japan, they try to make use of corporate resources to solve social issues, with the business boundaries of the company expanded. In case of Marui Group and Bridgestone, the effect of changing the internal and external boundaries of the organisation can be expected. The case of Mitsubishi Heavy Industries Group does not necessarily lead to a new business, but it is related to society in terms of utilising the social skills of members of the organisation, reshaping the border between the organisation and society.

In this book, we have distinguished infinite responsibility from finite responsibility and explained that ordinary business management is based on accountability as finite responsibility. However, the extent of accountability is not always fixed in practice. People work differently because the extent of accountability that every person recognises is different. Employees who have become aware of their infinite responsibility by participating in emergent responsible management can be expected to have a similar attitude towards their daily work. In dividing an objective and assigning it as 'responsibility', if the objective is fixed it is finite responsibility and it will disappear when the objective is achieved; however, the scope of responsibility becomes infinite if the objective continues to be reshaped. Employees who are awakened to their responsibility will be able to act in the same way in their work.

This is to understand responsibility as an active rather than a passive concept, and hopefully we can change the stereotype of 'responsibility' within an organisation. Compliance is one of the main issues of CSR, but corporate fraud is still on-going.

However, many incidences of corporate fraud do not happen intentionally, but are merely results of 'adjusting' practical 'differences' from laws and regulations by practitioners. In other words, it responds 'flexibly' due to the differences between the law and reality, subject to the judgement of the people concerned. Just regarding it as a rule violation would only encourage people to act in accordance with unrealistic rules. This would result in not only keeping out-dated rules, but also in increasing social costs and lowering efficiency, thus eventually destroying the pride of the human being. In such cases, the only fundamental solution is to point out that the laws and regulations do not fit the reality and then proceed to start revising them. To raise awareness of these issues, employees need to rely on their responsibility instead of the company's directions. If emergent responsible management is implemented based on infinite responsibility, it can be expected to be effective in addressing such problems.

12.5 Towards a New Connection

Accountability is past-oriented because it was defined and fixed in the past. On the contrary, responsibility is basically future-oriented, as it starts with searching for one's own responsibility. Fulfilling responsibility means cooperating not only with the person to be responded to, but also with those who feel the same responsibility. Certain fulfilled responsibility is always followed by another, thereby connecting responsibility persistently. This is similar to the connection in business, but strict conditions are imposed regarding whether it is economically feasible. Emergent responsible management is a model that creates new relationships and contributes to society by relaxing these economic constraints.

We do not insist that all activities be conducted based on emergent responsible management; neither do we claim that all social issues will be resolved by it. However, we contend that even if a company should take certain social responsibility, there are still issues that can only be addressed by emergent responsible management, and we have explored ways to achieve this in this book. Such activities should, in principle, be open to all employees. This is unquestionable because responsibility is imposed on all human beings.

This book has emphasised that responsibility is inherently subjective and focused on how to bring out the actors' spontaneity and facilitate emergent practice. However, whether to fulfil responsibility is not a matter of voluntary choice but an obligation. What should be judged voluntarily is how to fulfil one's responsibility. Therefore, emergent responsible management could not possibly be generalised unless the ethical understanding that it is an obligation to fulfil responsibility becomes widely spread. This may sound circular, but in order to promote such ethics, various practices of emergent responsible management are needed. This is the same as behaviour leading to habits and vice versa, but ethics as a social norm can only be fostered through such circulation.

Almost 20 years have passed since CSR emerged as a corporate practice and a governmental policy, but in many companies, CSR has been addressed as one of the company's normal operations with the most important aspect of responsibility being ignored. This is not only unfortunate for society and organisations but also for the people working in organisations. Emergent responsible management is a model that breaks such a barrier and creates a new connection, thereby transforming the organisation and society.

Correction to: Emergent Responsible Management

Katsuhiko Kokubu, Kimitaka Nishitani, Hirotsugu Kitada, and Mitsunobu Ando

Correction to: K. Kokubu et al., *Emergent Responsible Management*, Kobe University Monograph Series in Social Science Research, https://doi.org/10.1007/978-981-19-0416-5

The original version of the book has received belated corrections from the authors in Chapters 1, 2, 9 and 11, which have been updated. The book and the chapters have been updated with the changes.

Chapter ID	Page	Location	Error	Corrected
1	6	Note 4	Commission of the European Communities, Green paper: Promoting a European Framework for Corporate Social Responsibility	European Commission (2011) *Communication from the Commission to the European Parliament, the Council, the European Economic and Social Committee and the Committee of the Regions: A Renewed EU Strategy 2011–14 for Corporate Social Responsibility*, COM (2011) 681, p.6.
2	13	Par. 4	responsibility of an organization for the impacts of its […]	Responsibility of an organization for the impacts of its […]
2	15	Par. 3, line 4	[…] of the industry society.[4]	[…] of the industry society.

(continued)

The updated original version of these chapters can be found at
https://doi.org/10.1007/978-981-19-0416-5_1
https://doi.org/10.1007/978-981-19-0416-5_2
https://doi.org/10.1007/978-981-19-0416-5_9
https://doi.org/10.1007/978-981-19-0416-5_11

K. Kokubu et al., *Emergent Responsible Management*, Kobe University Monograph Series in Social Science Research, https://doi.org/10.1007/978-981-19-0416-5_13

(continued)

Chapter ID	Page	Location	Error	Corrected
2	17	Note 4	Absence of reference	Laloux, F. (2014) *Reinventing Organizations: A Guide to Creating Organizations Inspired by the Next Stage of Human Consciousness*, Nelson Parker, p.48.
9	93	Note 3	March, J. G and Simon, A.	March, J. G. and Simon, H.
11	120	Par. 4, line 4	'Porter Hypothesis	'Porter Hypothesis'

Afterword

The purpose of this book is to develop a new concept—*emergent responsible management*—and construct it as a new management model from both theoretical and practical perspectives. Whether the purpose of this book has been achieved or not depends on the reader's judgment, but since it is based on the concept of infinite responsibility which has not yet been discussed in the business world, it may be difficult to understand immediately. Hence, we again provide a summary of this book and answer some assumed questions in advance.

The central concept in emergent responsible management is infinite responsibility. From Chaps. 1 to 3, we have elaborated this concept and discussed how to apply it to the current management. To be specific, taking responsibility is supposed to respond to the call of others; thus, its scope is not essentially defined and should be infinite. It lies in the human nature of being willing to help those who are weak or in need. However, a company is an economic organisation, which is operated in a finite world that is always represented with monetary value. To pursue economic profits, companies are organised in a finite chain of responsibility, which is called accountability in this book. There are several ways to relate infinite responsibility to the dominant finite accountability in a corporate organisation. In this book, we have focused on corporate projects that pursue infinite responsibility and call it emergent responsible management.

The word 'emergent' is added because infinite responsibility is based on the response to others, thus emergent responsible management is characterised by emergent practice arising from the fusion of the self and others. Moreover, we suggest that a mechanism that brings out emergent practice is necessary for management. Another important feature of infinite responsibility is that the more we fulfil our responsibility, the more other responsibility will come out, and the more the responsibility becomes connected. Therefore, emergent responsible management has this feature of an autonomous movement that connects to external organisation, which is a 'social connection model'.

K. Kokubu et al., *Emergent Responsible Management*, Kobe University Monograph Series in Social Science Research, https://doi.org/10.1007/978-981-19-0416-5

After discussing these abstract concepts, we introduced examples of five companies from Chaps. 4 to 8. These companies do not mean to operate 'complete' emergent responsible management as defined in this book. Therefore, it is hard to say that they have practised perfect emergent responsible management. However, in this book, we intended to carefully extract the archetype of emergent responsible management from these activities. We emphasised corporate philosophy, solving social issues, and employees' spontaneity in the discussion. All of these three points are recognised by every company. The five companies show that emergent responsible management can succeed in practice if they integrate these elements well.

Therefore, proper management is necessary when considering these factors. For this purpose, Chaps. 9 and 10 discuss the organisational design and operational processes. This is a tentative study, but we tried to be as specific as possible with reference to the five case companies and the existing management theory.

The important point in the design of emergent responsible management is to construct a place where employees can play an emergent role more spontaneously. For this purpose, it is effective to balance the exploration and exploitation of knowledge; thus, it is necessary to clarify the roles of participants and share the issues. Furthermore, as an organisational activity, it is necessary to employ a mechanism that fosters employees' motivation to be spontaneous.

Regarding the operation process, we explained the differences between the systems for general management and emergent responsible management. It is possible to introduce a management system similar to the PDCA cycle even in emergent responsible management, but its operation should be implemented in exactly the opposite way. For example, goals and plans should be flexible, and it is fundamental to conduct self-evaluation if an assessment is required. The point is that while resembling the framework of the existing management system, the practice should be implemented flexibly so that the creativity of employees can be fully utilised.

Chapter 11 discusses how a company should conduct the SDGs initiatives as an application of emergent responsible management. If a company is committed to the SDGs, it should clarify its commitment and separate the activity from normal business activities. Infinite responsibility should work effectively when considering this commitment. The SDGs are goals and targets until 2030, but if goals are set as infinite responsibility, it will be continuously pursued by keeping the targets updated as finite responsibility, even after 2030. Therefore, there is great potential to pursue the SDGs as emergent responsible management.

Emergent responsible management is an activity that pursues infinite responsibility; thus, a company should not aim to earn profits from it. However, we do not deny that unexpected positive benefits may arise as a result of implementing it. These effects make a positive contribution to society. In Chap. 12, the effects of emergent responsible management are summarised, emphasising that the positive business effects must necessarily be secondary to the fulfilment of infinite responsibility.

A book usually only provides one-way communication, but we think it is our responsibility to respond to readers' call. As such, we will answer some assumed questions in advance. We hereby answer some assumed questions from business people and citizens who are interested in social issues regarding emergent responsible management. These questions were asked several times in our previous presentation in workshops and lectures.

A business person might ask, 'I understand the purpose of emergent responsible management, but is it able to survive in a tough competitive society?' Anyone working in a company may feel the same way.

A short answer to this question is that 'emergent responsible management is not a means used to survive competition'. It is understood that companies face intense competition in the current market environment. However, the primary purpose of a company is not to win the competition. Any company must have been initially organised to solve some social issues. Competition is only a condition for achieving its intended purpose.

However, with time going on and generations of management changing, people may tend to think that the continuation of an organisation is the primary purpose. To encourage employees who do not work hard, the boss sometimes threatens them, 'If you do not work hard, the company will be destroyed'. However, at that moment, we should realise that the purpose becomes making the organisation survive; thus, the people in such an organisation would have been reduced to simply being a means of doing something. The purpose of emergent responsible management is to reverse such a mind-set. Therefore, to survive the competition, we should employ other methods to strengthen management. The focus of this book is to clarify how to integrate such management with emergent responsible management and what the resulting effects will be.

In addition, a citizen who is interested in social issues asked, 'Is it possible to solve the current serious social issues by using emergent responsible management? How can we deal with urgent issues such as poverty eradication or climate change with it?'

The only answer to such a question is, 'If the problem is really a matter of urgency, it should be addressed in some other way'. Although emergent responsible management is an activity aimed at solving social issues, the assumed social issues present as responsibility to others, as recognised by individuals spontaneously, which may be different from those understood in society in general. However, it is important to be aware of such issues, which is the basis of responsibility.

Therefore, it is necessary to recognise that emergent responsible management is effective not because of its concrete effect of solving social issues but the continuous exploration of social issues. Responding with a small voice and even a silent voice makes the world easier to live in. Emergent responsible management is a practice that reacts to such a voice with corporate resources behind it.

Without a doubt, if poverty eradication or climate change is an urgent issue, we should address it as finite responsibility and even link it with laws and regulations if necessary. At such a time, how to deal with these assigned social responsibility and connect emergent responsible management with it will be important issues. This book did not fully discuss this issue but intended to address part of it in relation to the SDGs.

Jacques Derrida once exclaimed, 'There is no responsibility for the destruction of tradition, authority, legitimacy, rules, and doctrine, such as estrangement or creativity.'[1] The concept of infinite responsibility discussed in this book aims to break and recreate the current framework in practice. The new connections created by responsibility will revitalise, change the boundaries of organisations, and enable them to survive in society. Companies are economic organisations, but before that, they are organisations for people and by people, and if people were prior to the economy, it would be necessary to create human connections independent of the economy. Emergent responsible management is such an operation that restores connections from what tends to be concentrated on economic gains within a company to human-centred aspects. We wish that many companies could develop and spread their practices in a variety of ways.

[1] Derrida, J. (2004) *Shi Wo Ataeru (Donner La Mort)*, Chikuma (Japanese version), p. 61.

www.ingramcontent.com/pod-product-compliance
Ingram Content Group UK Ltd.
Pitfield, Milton Keynes, MK11 3LW, UK
UKHW022210051026
15624UKWH00001B/89

9789811904158